We Get to Carry Each Other

Other books by Greg Garrett from Westminster John Knox Press:

The Gospel according to Hollywood
Holy Superheroes! Exploring the Sacred in Comics, Graphic Novels, and Film (rev. ed.)
Stories from the Edge: A Theology of Grief

We Get to Carry Each Other

The Gospel according to U2

Greg Garrett

WESTMINSTER
JOHN KNOX PRESS
LOUISVILLE · KENTUCKY

1st edition
Published by Westminster John Knox Press
Louisville, Kentucky

09 10 11 12 13 14 15 16 17 18—10 9 8 7 6 5 4 3 2 1

Book design by Sharon Adams
Cover design by designpointinc.com
Cover illustration:© Reuters/CORBIS, file photo of Irish band U2 at
MTV European awards, Reuters/photo by Ferran Parades

Unless otherwise indicated, Scripture quotations are from the New Revised Standard Version of the Bible, copyright © 1989 by the Division of Christian Education of the National Council of the Churches of Christ in the U.S.A., and are used by permission.

Scripture quotations marked NJB are from *The New Jerusalem Bible*, copyright © 1985 by Darton, Longman & Todd, Ltd., and Doubleday, a division of Bantam Doubleday Dell Publishing Group, Inc. Reprinted by permission of the publisher(s).

Library of Congress Cataloging-in-Publication Data

Garrett, Greg.
    We get to carry each other : the Gospel according to U2 / Greg Garrett
    p. cm.
    Includes bibliographical references
    ISBN: 978-0-664-23217-7 (alk. paper)
    1. U2 (Musical group)—Religion. 2. Rock music—Religious aspects—
Christianity. I. Title.
    ML421.U2G37 2009
    782.42166092'2—dc22

               2009002875

For Martha Salazar: The Sweetest Thing

green press
INITIATIVE

Presbyterian Publishing is committed to preserving ancient forests and natural resources. We elected to print this title on 30% post consumer recycled paper, processed chlorine free. As a result, for this printing, we have saved:

14 Trees (40' tall and 6-8" diameter)
6 Million BTUs of Total Energy
105 Pounds of Greenhouse Gases
6,639 Gallons of Wastewater
224 Pounds of Solid Waste

Presbyterian Publishing made this paper choice because our printer, Thomson-Shore, Inc., is a member of Green Press Initiative, a nonprofit program dedicated to supporting authors, publishers, and suppliers in their efforts to reduce their use of fiber obtained from endangered forests.

For more information, visit www.greenpressinitiative.org

Environmental impact estimates were made using the Environmental Defense Paper Calculator. For more information visit: www.edf.org/papercalculator

Contents

Foreword

*M*aybe you've had a night like the one I'm remembering: I was staying at the home of a good friend in another state. It was late, with maybe a half-dozen people in the room, ranging in age from late teens to forty-something (you can guess which end of the spectrum I fit in). We got into a conversation about favorite songs, and my friend and his daughter, who had a good music collection between them, started pulling songs up and playing them as we mentioned them.

"Every Grain of Sand," by Bob Dylan, was my recommendation. We just sat and listened to the last sweet note.

Then someone suggested "Born to Run" by Bruce Springsteen, and again we sat and listened, the volume turned up high.

Then someone recommended another Dylan Song—maybe it was "Don't Think Twice"—and then it was "California" by Joni Mitchell, and then came songs by Sheryl Crowe and Sarah McLachlan and Bruce Cockburn, and then some other bands I hadn't heard of. It was my turn again, so I suggested "Why Worry" by Dire Straits, and then someone called for "Stop This Train" by John Meyer, and then someone said "Stuck in a Moment" by U2.

After the song ended, nobody spoke. After maybe a minute in that kind of rich, almost holy silence that we all experience sometimes, my friend's teenage daughter said, "Don't you feel lucky . . . so *honored* . . . just to be alive when these people are alive and creating their art?"

That late-night conversation came back to me as I read Greg's book, and with it, the joy of being alive while U2 is creating—not only their extraordinary music but also a movement of concern for global problems, especially in Africa. And Bono, in particular, is creating other things too. He's creating a different way of relating to people, not dividing the world into liberals and conservatives, but bringing together everyone he can from across the cultural/political spectrum for joint commitment to worthy goals. He's creating a different identity for what it means to be a rock star . . . known not for trashing hotels and generating tabloid scandals but for mobilizing public attention on the needs of hungry children and their sick parents and on other life-and-death emergencies around the world. And although he'd be quick to remind us that he's no Sunday school honor student, we might even say he is pioneering a different identity for being a Christian.

There are a lot of reasons to listen to music, but one of the best is that a good song is like a portal into a whole realm of human experience. When I finished Greg's book, I imagined groups of people—like the spontaneous listening party in my friend's living room—using this book to organize other listening parties. Greg gives a great song list at the beginning of each chapter, along with some worthwhile things to ponder, and participants could pull up lyrics online and go through portal after portal to think and talk about things that really matter.

I think U2 would be glad to know that sort of thing was happening through their songs. As a fellow author, I know Greg would be thrilled to see his book put to that good use. And I think every participant would remember those nights warmly for a long, long time, maybe for their whole lives. It might even help some of them get unstuck from a moment they can't get out of.

How about it?

Brian McLaren
Laurel, Maryland, 2009
(www.brianmclaren.net)

Introduction

The Gospel according to U2

Lookin' for to save my, save my soul.
Lookin' for the places where the flowers grow.
Lookin' for to fill that God-shaped hole.
"Mofo," from the album Pop[1]

Love, lift me out of these blues.
Won't you tell me something true.
I believe in you.
"Elevation," from the album
All That You Can't Leave Behind

"Religious freaks"

The rock band U2—bassist Adam Clayton, drummer Larry Mullen Jr., guitarist and keyboard player The Edge (born Dave Evans), and singer Bono (born Paul Hewson)—emerged from nowhere—almost literally. Dublin, Ireland, where the band formed in the mid-1970s, was not the bright, beating center of the entertainment world—not even when the writer Jonathan Swift had lived there, a couple of centuries earlier. U2 began with significant handicaps besides geography, not the least of which was that they were not yet, most of them, proficient musicians. But their youth, their energy, their intensity, their desire—these things set them apart from the very beginning, and from the beginning they thought that they were destined for greatness.

1

Rolling Stone writer Elysa Gardner wrote in her introduction to the magazine's book of collected articles on U2 that she first encountered these Irish upstarts in the early 1980s in the car of an "older, hipper friend" who was playing a mix tape of progressive music to aid in her musical education. In the midst of all this noise, she said that "Gloria," the first single from the band's second album, *October*, burst through as something magical, "everything the other songs on the cassette were ashamed to be: tender, urgent, vulnerable, resolute." When she asked who this band was, her friend had two identifiers ready: "They're from Ireland. . . . They're like, religious freaks, I think. But it's a great song isn't it? Powerful."[2]

So for this listener, it was an anomaly: They're religious freaks. But it's a great song, despite that.

For many years, this was my reaction as well. I had been following the Irish group many people call the greatest rock band in the world since the beginning of their career, had interviewed them, had felt my mind and spirit enlarged by them, but I never wanted to give credence to the idea that they were a Christian band.[3] As someone who had been badly burned by a Christian tradition in my youth, in the 1980s and 1990s I wanted my elevation and exhilaration free of religion—just as, conversely, some evangelical Christians really wanted to have their experience of transcendence affirmed by discovering that the grace they uncovered in U2's music was being mediated in familiar terms, by believing that they could claim members of the band as fellow travelers.

Now why should this have mattered to anybody? Well, partly it is because Christian culture, formed as it is by imperfect human beings, has sometimes done puzzling things. At its worst and most insular, it has elevated works that privilege message over form and safe subject matter over that which is difficult but inspiring, and it has sought confirmation that artists are within the safe walls of Christian orthodoxy before passing final artistic judgment. In the visual arts, for example, evangelical Christians acclaim the pretty but unchallenging paintings of Thomas Kinkade, the so-called "Painter of Light," because, as Kinkade claims, "they spread inherent life-giving values," while the harsh and challenging artistic vision of Andres Serrano's "Piss Christ" (a piece of art that some theologians suggest reflects the shocking humiliation of Christ's death on the cross) has been shunned and called blasphemous.[4] Similarly, in film, Mel Gibson's *Passion of the Christ* was seized upon by an enormous audience of evangelical Christians and devout Catholics who were told it was made by a Christian insider for Christian insiders, while *The Last Temptation of Christ* (a serious and even devout film directed by Martin Scorsese, who once wanted to be a Catholic priest), was banned and picketed by the Christian community for being—again—blasphemous.

One of the Christian responses to culture that H. Richard Niebuhr described in his landmark study *Christ and Culture* is the view that Christianity and the so-called secular culture should have no commerce, that "whatever may be the customs of the society in which the Christian lives, and whatever the human achievements it conserves, Christ is seen as opposed to them, so that he confronts men with the challenge of an 'either-or' decision."[5] While this is far from the only response to the question of how the life of the spirit and the culture might interact—and certainly not the response that the music of U2 and this book argue—it is a prominent, if (one hopes) no longer the dominant, response from American Christians.

But that's why this speculation about U2's religious faith (which, as you probably know, since you are holding this book about the gospel according to U2, turned out to be absolutely true) mattered (and matters) to so many Christians. For some of the students who talked with me about U2 in the 1990s in my office at Baylor University, one of the nation's largest Christian universities, establishing U2's Christian bona fides was essential. If members of U2 were indeed Christian, then their music was automatically certified; they could be listened to, their songs could be celebrated, and my students would not need to defend themselves against charges of apostasy or riotous living. But every time Bono used the "F" word in public, every time the band was seen cavorting in nightclubs, and when throughout the 1990s U2's music seemed to (and let's emphasize "seemed") celebrate the very culture they once shunned, the students' doubts began to rise: How could U2 be Christian if they acted like this?

At that time, I had the opposite concerns; imagining U2 to be Christian (as I then understood Christianity) threatened to diminish my love for the music. My exposure to other Christian artists and musicians had suggested that they were not so much artists as propagandists, pushing a message instead of following truth wherever it led them, and that certainly did not reflect my experience of U2 or of their music. So for as long as I could—until I myself became seriously religious—I ignored the "religious freaks" element of the band. It was a challenge, of course, since many of U2's songs reference the Bible, others speak of Christian faith, others critique the world's attachment to surfaces and superficial pleasures, and others preach justice, peace, love, and understanding in true gospel fashion. As Irish journalist Stuart Bailie understood long before I was willing to acknowledge it, spirituality was "the engine that drives the U2 machine," and their lyrics were "rich with the Psalms and Gospels," populated by "characters such as Judas and Noah."[6]

So, yes, it was a challenge, but like many other purely secular fans of the band, for some years I managed to ignore the spiritual content, the religious implications, and the theological questions bound up in the life and work of U2. I was able to soar with songs like "Where the Streets Have No Name," to draw comfort from songs like "Pride (In the Name of Love)," and to confront hard truths in songs like "Bullet the Blue Sky," to love the band without thinking too hard about what made their songs work and where they came from.

Or where they might lead.

I met U2 very early in their lives together. They were playing a club in Oklahoma City on a cold February night in 1982 when the band was touring behind *October,* and I was working for a music magazine as I put myself through college. Like many people, I had discovered U2 on MTV through the music videos for "I Will Follow" from *Boy* and "Gloria" from *October*, but since I had also bought *October* and worn out side one of the record when it was released in October of 1981, I was quick to volunteer when my editor asked for someone to cover the show.

U2 was playing Jammie's, a 300-seat club that was cavernous, low-ceilinged, and located in a rundown strip mall close enough to my apartment that I walked to the show, shivering. It was a horrible venue for live music, but the show itself was a transcendent vision: the band opened with "Gloria," launched into "I Will Follow" and "Out of Control," and not only brought the crowd to their feet but had them dancing and jumping on top of the tables, this supposedly objective journalist among them. By this time in my young journalistic career I had seen a lot of shows and interviewed some of the biggest rock bands of the day, but this young band from Ireland transfixed me. The energy with which they played, the vulnerability with which Bono interacted with the audience, and the band's almost-painful sincerity instead of the usual rock poses of irony and superiority transformed that dingy club into something that, if I'd been willing at that time in my life to consider it, I would have recognized: a place of worship.

During the time that U2 was playing, we in the audience were also transformed. We sensed our better natures, our connection to one another and to the world, and while they were playing, I honestly believed that—in the right hands—rock 'n' roll could change the world, because for an hour and a half, it had certainly changed us.

After the crowds cleared out, the staff started cleaning up and putting chairs up on tables, and Adam Clayton sat down to talk with me. My conversation was largely with Adam, although Bono and The Edge stopped by the table at various times. Adam and I were the same age—which was to say, in those days, very young (now, less so). He seemed tired, but I remember his confidence, his clear vision for the band, his willingness to engage my questions, which were almost ridiculously mundane after the transcendent show I had witnessed: How was the tour going? Did he think their youth was a help or a hindrance?

At one point while Adam and I were talking, Bono sat down at the table next to Adam. He leaned on his elbows toward me, and said—as apparently he often said to journalists, even back then—"You know, someday we're going to be the biggest band in the world."

The skeptical me, never far from the surface in those days, almost told him, "Sure you are," but I dutifully wrote down Bono's comment in my notebook, promptly forgot about it—and did not in fact recall it until 1987, five years later, when I picked up a copy of *Time* magazine, and saw Adam, Bono, and the rest of the band on the cover captioned "Rock's Hottest Ticket."

It is apparent to me now that U2 had a plan and a strategy from the very beginning. They were in this for the long haul, and the U2 story is now a given, a story with a shape that seems to us inevitable.

But it certainly did not seem inevitable on that night in 1982. Then I was just listening to young men talk about their hopes and dreams after one of the best rock 'n' roll shows of my life.

It's a sobering thing to imagine that the young men I met in that smoky club in Oklahoma City have since gone on to meetings with presidents and prime ministers. But even from the beginning, they had known about the transformative power of rock 'n' roll, properly applied. Their first gig together was as a band called Feedback. Bono reflected after that ragged show that he had given the audience all of himself, "gone for broke on the notion that they felt as he did, that *their* spirits were as alive as his was."[7] And their early passion was what I had felt in Oklahoma City, what has always made U2 a rarity in rock 'n' roll: that along with Bruce Springsteen, the Who, and a handful of other popular musicians, they were not in music just for what they could get out of it. Looking back over the three decades in which they've played, Bono recently said that what U2 brought from the very beginning was an emotional and spiritual rawness: "Rock 'n' roll is rarely raw in the emotional sense. It can be sexual, it can be violent and full of bile. Demons can appear to be exorcised, but they're not really, they're usually being exercised. The tenderness, the spirituality, the real questions that are on real people's minds are rarely covered." [8]

But that insight about what they were doing was developed through experience; it was not one they had all along. I did not realize it until years later, but during the time I was talking with Adam and Bono, U2 was just concluding a terrible crisis that had almost destroyed the band, a crisis having to do with the spirit. Bono, The

Edge, and Larry had been deeply involved with Shalom, a charismatic Christian community in Dublin. But after some time, the leaders of Shalom had made it clear that as they understood the Bible, Christian belief and pursuit of a career in popular music were antithetical—the either/or cultural option described by Niebuhr—and so U2 had two choices: they should either quit the band or leave the Shalom community.

At last, the religious members of U2 reached the conclusion that they could—and should—be a Christian rock band on their own terms, that their music and their faith could have a symbiotic relationship in which each fed the other—and both fed their audience. They left Shalom and organized religion behind. Still, the tensions between the Christian and secular worlds did not go away. Perhaps in a world that always tries to label things in order to understand them, they could not go away. Although U2 contains band members who are deeply religious, Bono, The Edge, and Larry turned away from organized religion because of their experiences with Shalom and because of the continuing religious clashes between Protestants and Catholics in their homeland. (As Larry noted, "The IRA would say 'God is with me. I went to Mass every Sunday.' And the Unionists said virtually the same thing. And then they would go out and murder each other.")[9] In America, we may have experienced "culture wars" that have created religious divides between us, but we have no real analogue for the violent heritage that the members of U2 observed growing up; it's easy to see how their opinions about organized religion might be colored by it.

And yet, out of this crucible—these tensions—they began creating ever more powerful music. After we talked, they went on to make albums like *War* and *The Unforgettable Fire* that engaged the political and the spiritual with insight and sincerity, and then they rose to worldwide acclaim (not to mention the cover of *Time*) with *The Joshua Tree*. They had shown the world that—for all intents and purposes—the spiritual life and success in rock music were not opposing values.

And then, in the 1990s, U2 went through a phase where some fans felt the band members had lost their faith, their bearings, or their minds.

Touring behind the powerfully dark album *Achtung Baby* and showcasing a character Bono played called "The Fly," U2 embarked on an ironic embrace of the culture and of their rock star status. Many U2 purists blanched at the sight of Bono in sunglasses (in which he remains to this day), at the spectacle and scale of the concerts, and at the band's musical embrace of dance and club music, while Christian fans of U2 were concerned about the songs themselves, which talked about sensation and consumption. Was "Miami" on *Pop* a hymn to mindless shopping, plastic surgery, and fashion? Was "Babyface" on *Zooropa* just another simplistic song about sex?

What those in panic mode did not understand, of course, was that U2 had not completely lost their minds; they had merely changed their methods. As The Edge pointed out, "We were always suspicious of irony, hiding behind a wink, clever-clever lyrics at the expense of soul. . . . But in retrospect, I think we followed that idea through to the end and actually discovered that irony is not necessarily the enemy of the soul."[10] There was some crisis of faith involved—The Edge says that this period was one of his spiritual low points, and Bono has described *Pop* as "a lover's row," an argument with God in the sense of the Psalms, honest dialogue with God.[11] But also, after the amazing success of *The Joshua Tree* and a resulting critical and popular backlash, the band decided that they had to change if they wanted people to go on listening to them. In a world full of excess, a world that celebrated irony (who can forget that the top-rated *Seinfeld* was, proudly "a show about nothing, with no hugging"?), no one seemed to pay attention to sincerity any more. But if you were excessive enough, you could, perhaps, draw people's attention to the fact of excess. So satire and irony, which U2 had always thought of as the enemies of authentic spiritual experience, became, for awhile, their tools to criticize the culture and point back toward a truth that might last.

And then, after *Achtung Baby, Zooropa,* and *Pop,* after two of the largest and most extravagant stage shows in rock history, U2 put away the drum machines and satire just in time to become the spiritual guides people needed in a post-9/11 world in which the religious extremism and violence U2 had known and condemned could—and did—strike people just like us. *All That You Can't Leave Behind, How to Dismantle an Atomic Bomb,* and *No Line on the Horizon* are albums for a world that needs sincerity again, a world prepared to ask the hard questions, especially if it's alongside a group of faithful people who have come to this place through hard questioning of their own.

U2's musical career and spiritual lives have this at their core: both ultimately are about people on a journey together. Many contemporary Christians have begun to recover the idea of the spiritual life as a pilgrimage rather than as a single moment of decision that includes some and excludes everyone else. Diana Butler Bass writes about this pilgrimage throughout her book *Christianity for the Rest of Us.* Today, she says, many Christians are "contemporary pilgrims on a quest to find home," and in their work, their public lives, and their spiritual lives, they are seeking meaning and understanding in the best ways they know how, with the help of fellow travelers along the way.[12] This could describe U2's journey as well, a journey that has been unlike many other rock bands because they're seeking different things than most of their peers, who flare up, flame out, and fade away. Steve Stockman, who wrote a book about the band's spirituality, said, "U2 didn't go into music for [the usual] reasons. They've never met the reason they got into it for. They're still journeying toward it, and I think that's why they're still making great albums."[13]

The band's most recent album, 2009's *No Line on the Horizon,* continues to wrestle with the concept of journey. The title is, *The Edge* reports, an image that grows out of the movement toward something that can't be perceived yet: "It's like when you're moving forward, but you're not exactly sure what you're heading towards—that moment where the sea and the sky blend into one. It's an image of infinity, I suppose—a kind of Zen image."[14] So even after thirty-plus years together, a lifetime in rock 'n' roll terms, U2 is still moving forward toward something it can't quite grasp, although they know that it's something bigger than they are, something beyond them. In that sense, *The Joshua Tree*'s "Still Haven't Found What I'm Looking For" is not a statement of doubt, but the quintessential account of faith. In the Christian tradition, we are told that we will never see fully until God makes all things known to us in God's own time. But we move forward, just the same, pilgrims on a journey, looking for a little elevation.

U2's journey is still in progress, but one thing does seem to have happened along the way: each of the band's members has bought into the life of the spirit. Even Adam, who was once on the outside of the religious troika, seems to have accepted the band's vocation and the reality of what they are. As he noted recently in talking about U2's creative process, "We are trying to pin down something elusive, something that represents where we are, emotionally, physically, spiritually."[15] All of those elements are important—and all of them go into making U2 who they are.

So at last, the surface tensions about Christianity and where it intersects with rock 'n' roll are only so important; what ultimately matters, and always has, is the music—those "great songs." *Rolling Stone* had said of the band as early as 1981, when only their first album, *Boy*, had appeared, that they were a band to be reckoned with, perhaps even "the Next Big Thing."[16] People— starting with those in the band—had thought so from the beginning. U2 were different—special, somehow—in the way they inspired and engaged. And this passion, spirit, and willingness to confront their own personal demons as well as the world's in songs that didn't sound like anyone else's was the primary reason people thought they might be destined for greatness.

Their music *mattered*.

And, of course, it still does.

Music That Matters

Almost everyone I know who loves U2 has stories. Edwin Beckham tells the story of seeing the show in Atlanta where Bono first introduced his father, Bob Hewson, to a large audience and Bob roundly cursed Bono because he didn't want to be singled out in such a big crowd. "I think he was a little drunk," Edwin says, smiling at the memory. Zane Wilemon, who was at one of the 2001 shows in Ireland at Slane Castle just after Bob Hewson died, tells how Bono came out in tears, how the audience pulled together as one to share his grief, how it was a healing time for everyone present—in that week just before 9/11, just before U2 went out and began healing the world. Sarah Dylan Breuer tells a story about being at a show that U2 closed with their contemporary psalm "40," how people had walked out of the building and into the streets still singing the refrain. Don Smith tells the story of being in Kenya with De Freeman, the two of them rushing someone to the hospital down the Great Rift Valley with U2 playing on the stereo, grounding them as they drove.

Almost everyone I know who loves U2 has stories. Something about them commands both affection and admiration. What they are doing in their music, in performances, and in the public sphere somehow causes people to identify them with holy and transformative times in their own lives, and somehow calls them to something higher and nobler.

Whatever it is U2 is doing, we might say, it is good news for many of those that encounter it.

"Good news" is the literal meaning of the Greek *euangelion,* which is usually translated as "gospel, " as in "the gospel according to." It doesn't mean "that which saves us," as some people mistakenly think, but it does mean a teaching, a proclamation, or an understanding that might change us, if we hear it and act on it. So what is the gospel according to U2? In particular, since we are dealing with a band in which spirit, music, and action are combined, what good news can U2 bring us that might help us to understand Christian belief and practice in a way that might transform our lives?

That's what we'll be examining in this book, and while clearly we'll want to save more complete discussions for later, I think we can make some preliminary identifications of some of the things that make U2 important. There's the music itself, the corresponding ideas of beauty and transcendence, the concept of the right notes, the right words, in the right places. "For U2," Bono says, "every night has to be the best night. . . . We have very high standards and we always remember who pays our wages. The audience deserves the best possible set of songs."[17] Unlike other musical superstars, some of whom continue to tour long past their ability to say anything important or new, seemingly just to keep up the payments on their castles, U2 is as committed to the process and the results as they were twenty-five years ago. That commitment has little or nothing to do with the need to earn a living. When, as they were making *The Unforgettable Fire*, they signed the record deal that would make each of them wealthy at the ripe old age of twenty-four, the band members recognized that this money could create the security they needed to go and do their best work, or it could throw everything out of balance. After the deal was announced, Bono told the band and its manager, Paul McGuiness, that money was corrupting, and that if they weren't careful it could separate them from their friends and from their roots. Simply put, "the deal was good news, but no reason to get carried away. They had a record to finish downstairs."[18] Their passion is not—and has never been—about the desire for what money can bring. It's centered solely on the music.

The beauty and truth U2 try to create in their music can lead us to some wonderful conclusions about creation, about praise for creation, and about a Creator that we will explore in chapter 1, where we will consider these and other lessons that U2 might teach us about faith and belief.

Second, there's the special chemistry between the four band members. While Bono, as the front man, has always been the most visible member and the main contact with the audience, each member of U2 serves a vital role musically and otherwise, and it has been this way from the beginning, ever since Larry Mullen Jr. posted an ad on a Dublin bulletin board seeking guitar players. He found Adam Clayton, who had a good-looking bass and amp and an air of confidence that he brought to the venture and transmitted to his fellows. He found Paul Hewson, also known as Bono Vox (which means "beautiful voice," although the name comes from a sign advertising a hearing aid), who wasn't much of a guitarist, or a singer, either, but who proved to have an incredible gift for connecting with an audience. And he found David Evans, The Edge, a guitarist just learning his craft, but whose interest in innovative sounds would shape the music of the fledgling band from the start.

Each member brought something unique and necessary to the band, something essential for its long-term success, and as in many successful communities, they have lived together, learned to love one another through good times and bad, and pushed one another to achieve great things. It's a stunning example of how four distinct individuals can form a community, and a reminder, as we will explore in chapter 2, of how necessary we are to each other. U2 certainly are a close fellowship, what in New Testament Greek is called a *koinōnia*. But, ironically, while the members of the group have run like the wind from membership in a traditional church, the band may also show us a powerful model of how a community of faith (what in New Testament Greek is called an *ecclesia*) ought to look and act.

Finally, there's the band's focus on real-world issues in their music and in their lives. The band has never shied away from writing songs about political and social issues. *The Unforgettable Fire*, for example, which proved to be a transitional album for U2 from the personal into larger issues, was inspired partly by an exhibition of art by survivors of the nuclear attacks on Hiroshima and Nagasaki. The paintings affected Bono deeply and turned into one of the underlying inspirations for the album's title track. Likewise, seeing one of his friends give up his life and soul to the cheap heroin that flooded Dublin in the late seventies and early eighties called forth "Bad." And the inspiration they found in the life and words of Martin Luther King Jr. led to "Pride (In the Name of Love)" and "MLK."

U2 has spent most of their career writing songs about things that have moved them personally, that have resonated with their faith understanding that we are called to be involved in the work of healing the world. But their life experiences also witness to this concern (and have indeed, often prompted it). Prior to the making of *The Joshua Tree*, Bono and his wife Ali went to Ethiopia to do volunteer work in a refugee camp where they saw the systemic effects of war and poverty firsthand. It opened him up personally to the things that he'd begun singing about and for which he'd been performing benefit concerts. "Ethiopia didn't just blow my mind," Bono told a journalist. "It opened my mind. On the last day at the orphanage a man handed me his baby and said please take him with you. He knew that in Ireland his son would live and in Ethiopia he would die. I turned him down. That was the rules. But in that moment I started the journey."[19] Asian wisdom tells us that each pilgrimage begins with a single step—and this first step led to insight not just for Bono but eventually also for all those who have heard the music that emerged from his journey.

Shortly afterward, Bono and Ali traveled to Nicaragua and El Salvador. They were shot at, witnessed the burning of villages, and saw the tangible results of American political policies in Central America. Bono, like the others in the band, loved America, which had welcomed them and believed in them, but now he began to understand that there were two Americas: the mythical America that Martin Luther King Jr. had dreamed about, and the actual America of Ronald Reagan, Nicaragua, and wretched excess. Bono said, "I wanted to describe this era of prosperity and Savings and Loans scandals as a spiritual drought." He talked about how in the wake of all he had seen, he felt he was finally "waking up as a writer and as a commentator on what I saw around me, my love of America and my fear of what America could become."[20] *The Joshua Tree* was the resulting album, and all of a sudden the whole world was listening.

The music and the lives that have grown out of these life experiences have called people to understand the inequity of systems that keep some people locked in poverty, the horrors of war, and the responsibilities of people of good will—these are the subject of chapter 3. We'll explore how a commitment to social justice is the logical result of belief and a spirituality lived out in community, and, perhaps, the only hope for the world.

So, our story so far: beauty, sincerity, a commitment to creating the best music possible, the power of communion, moral seriousness, belief in a better tomorrow—and there are other things as well, as we shall soon see. But this is plenty to launch us in the direction this book will travel.

I intend to take for granted that what people speak of when they talk about encounters with the sacred through U2's music are real and true, and that there are spiritual and theological explanations for those moments of transformation and transcendence. The current phenomenon of U2charists (that is, communion services built around the music of U2) are just the most formal manifestation of U2's engagement with the divine. In the process of discussing U2's songs, live shows, music videos, films, interviews, and social engagement, we will consider how U2 is indeed a Christian band, at least in terms of the questions they raise and the results they advocate. Those who see them are moved, challenged to be their best selves, comforted, attuned to injustice, even healed.

Perhaps U2 doesn't look (or sound) like most Christian musicians. But what could be more Christlike than what they do and what they produce? Jesus says throughout the Gospel of Matthew that people can be known by their "fruits," that is, the products of their lives:

> "Beware of false prophets, who come to you in sheep's clothing but inwardly are ravenous wolves. You will know them by their fruits. Are grapes gathered from thorns, or figs from thistles? In the same way, every good tree bears good fruit, but the bad tree bears bad fruit. A good tree cannot bear bad fruit, nor can a bad tree bear good fruit." (Matt. 7:15–18)

When we look at money raised for Katrina victims, hundreds of millions of dollars in debt forgiveness for Africa, people called to transformed lives of service, people elevated through their encounters with U2's music, people healed through communities forming around U2, then it seems to me that we're clearly seeing good fruits. So, as I said, I intend to take the spiritual element of U2's life and work seriously and to ask serious questions about where it might lead us in our own spiritual journeys.

What do the music, performances, and lives of U2 teach us about how we are to live, who we are, and what ultimately matters? (U2, after all, should be expert on what matters; back in 1985, *Rolling Stone* famously proclaimed them the band that matters most, perhaps even "the only band that matters.") What might explain the feelings that people associate with the band, its music, and its causes? Well, maybe Larry was onto something when he told *Rolling Stone* more recently that the way that people respond to U2 doesn't ultimately have anything to do with them, and that the band members have to remember that: "Something happens, but it is not something we can make happen. It only happens when God walks through the room."[21]

In my younger days, I thought that U2 could be accounted for purely as a secular phenomenon. Now, though, I understand that what *Rolling Stone*'s Elysa Gardner and I were hearing and loving in the music of U2 emerged precisely from what her friend demeaned: their honest quest for spiritual meaning in a world that pays lip service to the spiritual while chasing after the transient. While I would grant that in the past twenty-five years U2 has become musically innovative and rhythmically tight, while noting that their performances are packed with energy and spectacle, the heart of the band's appeal may finally lie in that spiritual quest, in their consciousness of the need to seek something greater than ourselves, and in their certainty that the shiny things this world has to offer us are only temporary expedients we use up in our ongoing pilgrimage toward the things that actually matter.

U2 and Theology

So we might say that U2 has become the biggest band in the world not in spite of their being "religious freaks"; they have achieved all this *because* of it. Band manager Paul McGuiness (the fifth Beatle, as it were, to the band) assured the band's members early in their career when they wondered if writing songs about faith made them freaks, "Look, these are not questions I'm asking, but they're questions I'm interested in. Anyone with a brain should be interested in these questions."[22]

U2's willingness to ask these questions has made them invaluable guides, and this book will take a look at the questions U2 has asked, at the provisional answers they have found and expressed along the way, and at what the wisdom tradition of Christianity (their tradition and mine) tells us about the issues they have considered. We call the field of inquiry in which U2 has opened these questions for us *theology*, which is one of the most off-putting

terms imaginable; to many people it suggests ivory-tower speculation, pointy-headed intellectuals with no interest in real life and
perhaps no interest in God either. But theology, as my bishop Andy
Doyle told me recently, is really just "God-talk, and our willingness to have it."[23] And while we may think (or be encouraged to
think) that theology is something better left to the intellectuals, to
the leaders of the church, to people somehow smarter or more
faithful or more grounded than us, theology is a vital practice, intimately related to our everyday lives, and infinitely necessary, particularly if we are people of faith—or long to be.

I have great admiration for the current archbishop of Canterbury, Rowan Williams, who is a towering intellect and a person
of deep spiritual understanding, just the sort of person we imagine "should" be doing theology. But what Williams tells us is that
any "person shaping their life in a specific way, seeking disci-
pline and consistency in relation to God" is doing theology, and
that "the believing artist or liturgist or hymnographer is likewise
engaged in a theological task."[24] So when we engage in God-talk,
either by asking formal questions or by faithfully making art (or
both, as U2 sometimes does), we are doing theology, and the
questions will lead us toward provisional answers that will shape
our lives. Of course, our understanding of God is always imperfect, and thus our understandings of how we are supposed to
relate to that God and shape our lives around that God are likewise only provisional. But constantly asking the questions is a
vital part of doing and being what we are called to in this life, and
U2's answers may give us strength, comfort, and wisdom—or
may have already done so.

So what are these questions that Paul McGuiness said were so
important? Although our popular conception may be that theology
seeks irrelevant information like "How many angels can dance on
the head of a pin?" or "Can God create a rock so heavy he can't
move it?" I'd like to suggest a simplified and relevant set of questions that I think the members of U2 have asked and, over the past
three decades, begun to answer for themselves, four questions that
might go on to indicate the importance of theology for us and for
the world around us:

What do I believe about God?
Who are my companions in belief?
How can my belief transform me?
How can my belief transform the world?

In the music of U2, in the words they have spoken, and in the lives they have lived, we see the band responding to these four questions, sometimes unconsciously, but often with extreme deliberation. In the chapters that follow, we will trace their developing answers to these questions. These four questions also convey a multitude of subquestions, of course, some of which we'll pursue, but we'll try to confine ourselves to those where U2 has already opened the door for us to poke our heads in and look around.

In taking U2 seriously as theologians and seekers of truth, I am—more than most people—cognizant of the voices from both sides of the divide that will resist that enterprise. Some Christians will argue that God's revelation already comes through perfectly good religious channels: in the reading of the Bible, perhaps, or through trained theologians, or in the inspired preaching or teaching of ministers of the church. *Why should I imagine I'm going to discover sacred wisdom from rock stars?* Meanwhile, some in secular culture will argue that in laying our hands on the work and persons of U2, we are doing religious violence to them, trying to appropriate them for our Christian cause when their music works perfectly well for nonbelievers, thank you. *Why should I have to be Christian—or acknowledge their Christianity—to appreciate U2?*

Since I have lived in each of these worlds, I can explain that my reasons for writing this book are personal, spiritual, and pragmatic. This book is personal because U2 has been an important part of my own spiritual journey, so I know a little something about the effect they have on people who love their music. In the years when I was outside of belief and Christian community, the music of U2 was one of the things that made me feel life might be worthwhile and that there might be something larger out there if I could just get my hands around it. Like the songs of Bruce Springsteen (who nightly shouts out into darkened arenas, "Is there anybody alive out there?"), U2's music let me know I was not alone and that there was something more than just darkness, if I could only hang on.

"Beautiful Day" especially carried me through some of my ugliest days, and I lived in hope that my own personal flood might be followed by a rainbow.

Without U2's powerful music, hopeful words, and the larger sense of community that their music held out to me in my worst times, I honestly might have found myself stuck in a moment I couldn't get out of. So I want to acknowledge that this music has been personally important to me, and to others I know and love. I thought that a book taking U2 seriously, as I promise to do, could give others permission to claim the comfort and wrestle with the personal transformation that many of these songs invite.

I think of this book as spiritual, because, as the band, critics, and I have suggested, U2's music revolves around deep spiritual questions; even the love songs point us to larger realities, desires, and concerns. Throughout their career, including in the supposedly decadent days of "Zoo TV" and "Pop Mart" in the 1990s, U2 has always made music about "spiritual search, and conscience and commitment," as critic Jay Cocks argued in his cover article for *Time*.[25] Eugene Peterson, one of Bono's favorite spiritual guides, would second this. He has described attending a so-called "Evening of Jesus and Bono" where even those who were not Christians (the majority of the audience) felt connections "because Bono had engaged them at some level of spirit more authentic than the culture of addictions and consumerism they were accustomed to living in."[26] Like Peterson, I take U2's spiritual nature seriously because it seems to reflect much of what I understand about faith and faithful action.

Finally, this is a pragmatic work because it seems clear to me that in what is rapidly becoming a postmodern and post-Christian society, the powerful narratives of God and Christianity are not being told by the institutional church as successfully as Christians might hope. Instead, contemporary popular culture—our movies, music, video games, television shows, and other storytelling media—have become, for many people, the place where they seek and find meaning for their lives. I, too, have experienced holy moments in movie theaters and concert halls.

Many people don't want to consider the idea that Christian

practice and proclamation have lost any of their ability to engage the world, and they certainly don't like the idea that ultimate meaning may now be transmitted to many people through iPods and Xboxes. U2's music shows both why this paradigmatic shift could be disastrous—Is the shiny consumerist culture that they sing about satirically in "Miami" good for anything but momentary satiety on the way to continuing misery?—but why it can also be a source of light and hope. Has anyone, for example, written a more stirring song about the gospel mandate to seek peace than their "Peace on Earth?" It may in fact be true that, as Kelton Cobb notes, the "biblical stories, paradigmatic figures in the church, sanctioned ritual actions and symbols, and the essentials of the creeds" are no longer primary makers of sacred meaning in our culture, especially for younger people, and that many of us are now leaning on "pop music and other storytelling media [to find] the narratives of our lives that are most convincing to us, that best make sense of our lives," and that express our ethical understandings.[27]

This could certainly be a very bad thing—and often is when artists either fail to ask the important questions or celebrate only those things that are self-serving and of the moment. I for one do not want my eleven-year-old learning his ethical lessons or only making sense of his life through the medium of the American idols of the day. But our current reliance on popular culture for life narratives could be a positive thing if it is possible that, as Richard Niebuhr also wrote, Christ can transform culture into a vehicle of sacred meaning through the hands of people "living in a created world," and creating by "the creative power and ordering of the divine Word," or if, as Paul Tillich argued, in secular culture there is still a "Latent Church" where "the ultimate concern that drives the manifest Church is hidden under cultural forms."[28] (It may also be true, as Bono said in the early 1980s, simply that each of us has his or her job to do, and in the "battle between good and evil," one's job "may be on the factory floor, or it may be writing songs.")[29]

Not all cultural artifacts express sacred and profound wisdom; I would be the first to acknowledge that most do not. But if we can pay attention to the culture when it does, then I believe it can be a powerful source of revelation for us. Bono once said, "I'm only interested in artists that I learn from by what's happening in their experiences and their life."[30] When a band like U2 asks important questions—when in their experiences and their lives they find answers that we can learn from, answers that can profitably open up aspects of our spiritual traditions—they can become a vehicle for meaning that speaks into a contemporary vacuum. They can remind us of those things that we have lost, encourage us to dig deeper, and recover for us what drew people to faith traditions in the first place: community, transcendence, and ultimate meaning.

Maybe it's true that, as Bono often says, he's no theologian, if by that we mean a professional theologian (whatever that rare beast might be these days). But as Jason Byassee wrote in *Christian Century*, they are doing the work nonetheless: "The members of U2 are genuine theologians who have digested the scriptures and reiterate them in their songs. . . . They speak in parables, offering discourse about the soul for those with ears to hear."[31] In their music, the members of U2 are doing theology—and often in what they say and how they live they do it as well.

So read with skepticism, if you will; I would expect nothing less. If something makes sense to you, try it on as a provisional meaning. If something doesn't, then keep looking. What has made U2 so popular has been described in all sorts of ways that have nothing to do with spirit or religion or theology: cultural explanations, market explanations, aesthetic explanations. These are important, but ultimately they fail to do justice to U2's almost universal appeal. U2 has succeeded as only a handful of popular artists ever have because through the beautifully crafted medium of their art, they call us to something larger than ourselves, to our own best selves, and to action that makes a difference in the lives of others.

N. T. Wright had a novel idea that I would love to imagine in practice: "If all theology, all sermons, had to be set to music, our teaching and preaching would not only be more mellifluous; it might also approximate more closely to God's truths, the truth revealed in and as the Word made flesh."[32] In these pages, we'll examine how U2 teaches and preaches and does theology that is set to music, and does it in ways that can illuminate our lives and shape a better world.

Chapter One

Belief

"All Because of You, I Am"

Listening File

Before (or while) reading this chapter, listen to these U2 songs. If you have an iPod or other digital music player, you may want to create a playlist or folder containing these songs and set it on repeat.

You can access lyrics for all U2's songs on U2's official Web site: u2.com.

"I Will Follow," *Live from Boston* (originally from *Boy*)
"Gloria," *October*
"Pride (In the Name of Love)," *The Unforgettable Fire*
"40," *War*
"Drowning Man," *War*
"When Love Comes to Town," *Rattle and Hum*
"Mysterious Ways," *Achtung Baby*
"Grace," *All That You Can't Leave Behind*
"All Because of You," *How to Dismantle an Atomic Bomb*
"Yahweh," *How to Dismantle an Atomic Bomb*

Prayer and Belief

In February of 2006, President George W. Bush and Jordan's King Abdullah II joined senators, members of Congress, and three thousand other political movers and shakers who gathered at the

23

Washington Hilton for an interfaith gathering known as the National Prayer Breakfast. U2's lead singer, Bono, was also present at the prayer breakfast, but he did more than just attend; at the appointed time, he strode to the podium (or the pulpit, if you prefer), and he began to preach.

The first thing he acknowledged to these political leaders from Christian, Jewish, and Islamic faith traditions was the possible cognitive dissonance involved in his standing in front of them:

> If you're wondering what I'm doing here, at a prayer breakfast, well, so am I. I'm certainly not here as a man of the cloth, unless that cloth is leather. And it's certainly not because I'm a rockstar . . . the reason for this gathering is that all of us here—Muslims, Jews, Christians—all of us are searching our souls for how to better serve our family, our community, our nation, our God. I know I am. Searching, I mean. And that, I suppose, is what led me here, too.[1]

To many fans of the band—and to those who have followed the life and work of U2—the idea of Bono at a prayer breakfast is not so strange, of course. Bono, The Edge, and Larry were once members of a charismatic Christian group that immersed them in prayer and Bible study, and the three have continued to be people of faith after leaving the Shalom community, even though they have lived that faith largely outside of church walls. Bono has said that he is a great believer in prayer, and some of the music the band made during that period when they were struggling with how to be both faithful Christians and faithful musicians ("Gloria" and "Rejoice" from the *October* album, for example) can actually best be understood as prayer.

The truth is, from that time to this, U2 has been making music that relates a speaker's approach to God, expresses fears and hopes to God, and demonstrates the desire for connection to the divine. And that, according to George Appleton, is what prayer is: "man standing before his maker in wonder, awe, and humility; man, made in the image of God, responding to his maker."[2]

Prayer is also, as Frank Griswold (the past presiding bishop of the Episcopal Church) says, about relationship, and relationship implies two (or more) entities in communication and communion. When I pray, I am standing—or kneeling—here. Who or what is there receiving my prayers?

So prayer implies someone who hears, and, perhaps, responds in some way to that prayer, and this leads us into the realm of faith and belief. What we think we understand about prayer suggests much about the One to whom we pray.

The seventeenth-century English Puritan John Bunyan defined prayer in a way that may open useful doors for us as we think about relationship, faith, and belief. Bunyan, who wrote several books on prayer, said that "prayer is a sincere, sensible, affectionate pouring out of the heart or soul to God, through Christ, in the strength and assistance of the Holy Spirit, for such things as God has promised, or according to his Word, for the good of the church, with submission in faith to the will of God."[3] Prayer, Bunyan suggests, involves a relationship to God where the one praying pours out her heart; Jesus and the Holy Spirit are in the neighborhood, somehow; God has a relationship with us that involves promise or covenant; God seeks good for those who believe in him, good expressed through the Christian community; and God is ultimately the member of this conversation who gets to decide what happens. We'll explore all of these things, but let's begin with some specific song prayers from U2 to see what they might suggest about the God they posit.

The song "40" from *War* is one of the best examples in the U2 canon of prayer in the form of pop music. The song sets to music the first three verses of Psalm 40, which go as follows:

> I waited patiently for the LORD;
> > he inclined to me and heard my cry.
> He drew me up from the desolate pit,
> > out of the miry bog,
> and set my feet upon a rock,
> > making my steps secure.
> He put a new song in my mouth,
> > a song of praise to our God.
> Many will see and fear,
> > and put their trust in the LORD.[4]
>
> (Ps. 40:1–3)

What does "40" tell us about the God to whom it is directed? The speaker imagines a God who listens, who strengthens, who inspires—a familiar figure of God to those who know and love the Psalms, the ancient hymnal of the people of God. Bono has acknowledged that the book of Psalms is perhaps his favorite book, and that these ancient prayers were part of his first real experience of God:

> Psalms and hymns were my first taste of inspirational music. I liked the words, but I wasn't sure about the tunes—with the exception of Psalm 23, "The Lord is my Shepherd." I remember them as droned and chanted rather than sung. But they prepared me for the honesty of John Lennon, the baroque language of Bob Dylan and Leonard Cohen, the open throat of Al Green and Stevie Wonder. When I hear these singers, I am reconnected to a part of me I have no explanation for—my "soul" I guess.
>
> Words and music did for me what solid, even rigorous, religious argument could never do—they introduced me to God, not belief in God, more an experiential sense of GOD.[5]

"40" was composed at the end of recording sessions for the *War* album. Bono remembered that the band wanted to conclude with "something explicitly spiritual on the record to balance the politics and romance," and the song is awash with reverence for a God who rescues and brings new hope.[6] From the "War" tour through 1990's "Lovetown" tour, U2 used the song in the same way they employed it on the album, to close their shows simply, spiritually, and with quiet passion. The group slowly left the stage one by one, while the audience continued to sing, "How long to sing this song?" The song was shelved during the "Zoo TV" and "Pop Mart" era, when the song's simplicity and earnestness would have seemed out of place, but the band again began closing shows with "40" during the "Elevation" tour.

"Yahweh," from *How to Dismantle an Atomic Bomb,* is another sung prayer we could think of as a contemporary psalm, one actually directed to God by name. "Yahweh" is (we think) the proper name of the God of Abraham and Sarah, the God of the Prophets, the God we still worship today. The prophet Amos described him in this way:

For look, he it is who forges the mountains, creates the wind,
who reveals his mind to humankind,
changes the dawn into darkness
and strides on the heights of the world:
Yahweh, God Sabaoth, is his name.

(Amos 4:13 NJB)

The name "YHWH" (as it is spelled in Hebrew, which has no vowels), is used over six thousand times in the Hebrew Bible (or Old Testament), although many translations follow the Jewish practice of not saying the name of God, and so render it simply as "Lord." Its meaning is uncertain, although many scholars believe "Yahweh" to be an ancient form of the verb "to be," which might explain why, when Moses asked the Voice in the burning bush who it was, he got this reply: "God said to Moses, 'I AM WHO I AM.' He said further, 'Thus you shall say to the Israelites, "I AM has sent me to you"'" (Exod. 3:14).

The song "Yahweh" is musically direct and simple (and even more so in concert, when The Edge breaks out his Taylor acoustic for the only time in the set and the band skips the bridge section). This musical simplicity matches the straightforward address of the Lord: "Yahweh, Yahweh." The lyrics, in which the singer asks God to take all that is broken or unclean about him and repair it and to redirect him in the ways that he should go, acknowledge Yahweh's creative and transformational power and seem to assume a particular relationship between singer and Creator:

Take these shoes
Click-clacking down some dead end street.
Take these shoes
And make them fit.
Take this shirt
Polyester white trash made in nowhere.
Take this shirt and make it clean, clean.
Take this soul
Stranded in some skin and bones.
Take this soul
And make it sing.

The singer also asks for God's blessing—a kiss on those lips of his that are too quick to criticize—and concludes with the plea to be broken before God as part of his path to transformation. The coming dawn and the child waiting to be born in the repeated chorus symbolize this transformation, which in the Christian tradition we sometimes call *metanoia*.

Who is the God implied in "Yahweh"? Again, it is a God in relationship with the one who prays as well as a God who cares for us too much to allow us to remain the way we are. These are familiar sentiments from the Judeo-Christian understanding, as we've seen in the Psalms. Another parallel contemporary response is suggested by these prayerful words directed to God (which I've laid out in verse form to emphasize the parallels; the original is in prose) by the Catholic mystical writer Thomas Merton:

> Untie my hands and deliver my heart from sloth. . . .
> Give me humility in which alone is rest . . .
> deliver me from pride which is the heaviest of burdens . . .
> possess my whole heart and soul with the simplicity of love. . . .
> For there is only one thing that can satisfy love and reward it,
> and that is You alone.[7]

Psalms of Pain and Praise

So far, we've seen examples of song/prayer that suggest a faithful God, a responsive God, a saving God. Some prayers are joyful; others ask questions. In the Judeo-Christian tradition, prayers often come from people who are angry, sad, or frightened, and who want to know where God is in all of that. Many of the Psalms ask God why he has not acted, when he will come and rescue the speaker, how long the psalmist will have to sing this song. The Hebrew tradition in particular is full of lamentation, where a speaker cries out to God or even takes God to task, a practice that makes many Christians feel uncomfortable.

This may explain some of the reactions faithful people had to the album *Pop*: while we're all looking to fill the God-shaped hole "Mofo" reminds us about, some of the songs on that album seemed so dark, so angry, so, well, faithless. Bono acknowledged that the album could be said to be about the so-called death of God (or the absence of God). Although the songs were not Bono's own personal questions, he said, "I felt they were in the minds of a lot of people around me."[8] Doubt, fear, and anger are rarely acknowledged by people of faith—despite the fact that the Hebrew Bible and even the Christian Testament contain many examples of it. If we imagine prayer as relationship, then it may sometimes acknowledge that at least one person in the relationship doesn't feel things are going particularly well at the moment. Many of the Psalms do, in fact, which is perhaps why Bono said that the songs on *Pop* were very much in the tradition of the Psalms. They still believe, even if they don't understand the God they question.

Pop's "If God Will Send His Angels," was, Bono said, another song about the relationship that wasn't going well, "A song of quiet anger at the way the world is and God's failure to intervene." But the entire album, he says, could be called "Shouting at God": "There are a lot of arguments with God on this record. . . . But it does not chart my loss of faith . . . if you're rattling on and on about how much you don't love somebody, it is evidence of passion. You can't be having an argument with God if you don't believe there is one."[9]

So prayer, pleading, even shouting at God implies relationship, and relationship, when we speak of God, brings us back to belief. In "Rejoice," from *October*, we come close to the lament tradition of the Hebrews, as embodied in some of the Psalms and in the book of Lamentations. The sense of the song is this: *I do not understand the things that are happening around me, and I call out to God. I don't see things changing—and yet I believe, because of my understanding of God, that they will change someday. He is God, so he must know what he is doing. And so, I rejoice.* As the song says,

> And what am I to do?
> What in the world am I to say?
> There's nothing else to do.
> He says he'll change the world some day
> I rejoice.

What is the vision of God suggested by this prayer? A God of perfect wisdom and perfect justice. A God who will not allow things to remain such a mess forever.

So if this represents our authentic belief, our only possible response to life is to rejoice (as also in "Gloria," a twentieth–century "Glory to God in the Highest!"), for God is God, and we are not, and in all things, we trust that God is working toward the perfection of the cosmos (as Bunyan said, we pray "with submission in faith to the will of God"), and so God must be praised.

Bono's theological understanding when he wrote these songs does not seem to match the more mature understanding he and the band reach later (remember, this song emerged while he, The Edge, and Larry were still part of a conservative charismatic Christian group emphasizing personal piety). The song justifies a certain passivity: "I can't change the world / But I can change the world in me / If I rejoice." As we will see later, U2's shift from a focus on personal piety to a more active partnership with God makes these lines seem a bit archaic, yet it does lead us in the direction of good spiritual practice. Wisdom traditions from around the world argue that we must be transformed before we can reach out to others, and certainly it is true that all things are ultimately in the hands of God; the God revealed in this prayer is one with the power to change things even if they are beyond our power.

For over two thousand years, the Psalms have been the prayerful songbook of God's people, so it's not surprising that we should find song and prayer fitting together so naturally. Listening to "Rejoice" reminds us of the power of music in spiritual practice. Many of the Psalms (including Ps. 40) call for us to sing and play instruments, for Yahweh is always worthy of our highest praise:

> Rejoice in the LORD, O you righteous.
>   Praise befits the upright.
> Praise the LORD with the lyre;
>   make melody to him with the harp of ten strings.
> Sing to him a new song;
>   play skillfully on the strings, with loud shouts.
>   (Ps. 33:1–3)

The combination of music, words, and rhythm in "Rejoice" (and many other U2 songs, of course) combine to create an effect much greater than the words alone. In fact, words are inadequate for the kind of rejoicing these songs are doing, and certainly inadequate to the task of speaking that which is beyond words, as the words themselves admit. In "Rejoice," Bono sings, "And what am I to do? / What in the world am I to say?" while in "Gloria," the singer repeats, "I try to sing this song," acknowledges "I try to speak up / But only in you I'm complete," and pleads "Lord, open my lips." In the end, only the ancient Latin words of worship are sufficient. The God revealed in these songs is not only worthy of praise but so exalted that it is difficult to find adequate words.

Ultimately, these songs sound like the kind of pure praise that Augustine spoke about in his work on the Psalms, *Ennarrationes in Psalmos*:

Singing to God properly is singing "with jubilation." Now what is this singing with jubilation? Think of people singing as they go about some hot and exhausting job. . . . They start celebrating in their happiness with the words of familiar songs. But they end up turning away from words and syllables, as if they were filled with so much happiness that they couldn't put it into words. And off they go into the noise of "jubilation" . . . a sound which means that the heart is giving birth to something it cannot speak of. And who better to receive such "jubilation" than the ineffable God—ineffable because you cannot talk about Him. And if you cannot talk about Him, and it is improper just to keep silence, why, what is there left for you to do but "jubilate"?[10]

Bono seems to understand jubilation (a word he repeats joyfully over and over again when performing the song "Elevation") in the same way; it is almost as though in these and other songs, U2 is putting Augustine's words into practice.[11] Reviewers actually sometimes refer to Bono's use of "oh" as an inarticulate but jubilant response to what cannot be put into words. Despite those who are skeptical about U2's faith and practice, in this regard they are undeniably Christian in their understanding. Walter Brueggemann has written that "our faith . . . is not about pinning down moral certititudes. It is, rather, about *openness to wonder* and *awe in glad praise* [italics his]."[12] (It is about other things as well, as Brueggemann would be the first to acknowledge, but it is certainly about these things we find in U2's music.) God is powerful, exalted, and elevated, and perhaps only through pure praise can we express what we feel and know and believe about this God.

So "40," "Yahweh," "Rejoice," and other examples of song as prayer in the U2 canon (and I do not count here, although I might, the transcendent experience that audiences might compare to prayer as they watch, shout, and sing these and other songs at a U2 concert) confirm us in thinking of at least some of U2's music as prayerful, which, as we've observed, opens up significant questions. When we pray, to whom are we praying? What are we praying for? Why do we expect our prayers to be heard? What results should we expect? All of these are theological questions relating to the nature of God.

The Nature of God

In a recent speech that he began by quoting Bono on religion, the Archbishop of Canterbury Rowan Williams said, "To discover who I am I need to discover the relation in which I stand to an active, prior Other, to a transcendent creator: I don't first sort out who I am and then seek for resources to sustain that identity."[13] Prayer is theological because it assumes an idea of God and a relationship with God, and that relationship helps us to know who we are and what we are called to do.

As we saw, U2's prayers—and songs asking God hard questions—assume ideas of God and relationships with God: *God is relational. God is loving. God wants to transform us. God wants to elevate us. God seeks justice. God is merciful. God is worthy of praise.*

Although some Christians think of U2 as unorthodox or even unchristian, the ideas of God suggested by U2's music and words are completely orthodox, a word that comes from the Greek word *orthodoxos,* meaning "right belief or opinion"; to be orthodox is to be within the main tradition of belief. Even some of the most challenging notions expressed about, to, or against God in U2's music are, as we noted, a historical part of the Judeo-Christian tradition, so in this, too, they are in the mainstream of belief.

At its heart, U2's understanding of God appears to conform to the understanding of God we find in the most orthodox document of mother church, the Nicene Creed, which proclaims that we believe in God, the Father, the Almighty; in Jesus Christ, his only Son, our Lord; and in the Holy Spirit, the Lord and the Giver of Life. What we find in U2's music and described by their words and lives is the triune God known in most Christian understanding: God the Father, God the Son, and God the Holy Spirit.

The Trinity (the idea that the one supreme God is experienced in three distinct persons) is a challenging and, for some, ridiculous theological concept, but music actually provides better opportunities to understand it than words alone. English musician and theologian Jeremy Begbie often talks about the Trinity at the piano as he plays a chord—three notes, audible and capable of being played separately but creating something of real beauty when they're sounded together. Simultaneously we hear three individual notes and the combination of them into rich harmony.

Our experience of the band U2 likewise has some of those same paradoxical qualities of individuality and mingled group identity that could help us understand the concept of the Trinity. U2 can be talked about as an entity, as I have been doing (and will continue doing) throughout the book: U2 *is*. It can be spoken of as a unity. But U2 also *are* The Edge, Adam Clayton, Larry Mullen Jr., and Bono, four distinct people with diverse talents and varied appearances who act differently, speak differently, and make their way in the world differently. What happens at a U2 concert may be the best way to understand this dance between unity and diversity we call "Trinity" (*perichoresis*, the "Dance of God," is a term sometimes used to explain the interaction of the persons of the Trinity): the four people who stand onstage performing separate functions play and sing, speak (or don't speak), move, pose, reach for the audience: Bono, The Edge, Adam, and Larry.

And yet what makes the experience "U2" are those separate functions combined with beauty and grace and love into something so much larger than the individual parts. Larry in fact describes U2 as a sort of holy mystery: "We are four very, very different people with diverse personalities. . . . We are one, but we are definitely not the same . . . what happens when we get together on stage or in the studio. It's very hard to describe and even harder to explain. . . . When we play music together, something happens."[14] It is something miraculous—a dance in which they are simultaneously individuals and joined in union; if we look at them separately, we can see them separately, but we also see them all at once, together, and that is how we are most powerfully affected by them.

Our understanding of ourselves in relation to others begins with our understanding of a God who exists in community, of a unity that also can be understood through separate functions, roles, or persons. So it is in the Trinity: The Father creates, the Son redeems, the Spirit sustains. The Father *is*; the Son *does*; the Spirit *loves*. And, at the same time, there is only one God.

Theologians have long made logical defenses of the concept of the Trinity, but ultimately Trinity is a mystery, one of those things that requires, as Anselm of Canterbury says, faith seeking understanding (or, as in "Walk On," perhaps Trinity is "a place that has to be believed to be seen.") It's a challenging concept if we rely purely on logic. But since U2 understands God to be a Trinity, we will need to wrestle with the theological concept—and who knows? Maybe we will uncover some truths about God that will open up new vistas for you.

Let's begin in the logical place—with God the Father. The God who is being called on to transform the singer in "Yahweh," the God who is praised ("gloria") and exalted ("exaltate") in "Gloria," and the God who will "change the world some day" in "Rejoice" contain familiar aspects of the person we call God the Father. As Henry O. Thompson notes, Yahweh is identified in many ways in the Hebrew Bible:

> He is a storm god who speaks in the thunder, who hurls or shoots lightning (Exod 19:16–19; 20:18; Ps 18:14; Job 37:5; Amos 1:2; Hab 3:11). He is a god of the mountains (Exodus 19; 1 Kgs 20:3). . . . He is a god of the desert (Judg 5:4). He has control

over the waters of the earth—the sea (Exod 14:21; Jonah), the rivers (Josh 3:16–17), and the rain (Gen 2:5; 1 Kings 17). He is the giver of life and one who brings death. He is a god of war and of peace. But most important to the biblical tradition, Yahweh is the god of the covenant.[15]

All of that is to affirm that the God revealed in the Hebrew Bible is powerful, relational, worthy of praise, and moving history toward some good conclusion. This is the Yahweh or God the Father identified for us by U2's prayer/songs, the all-powerful God who nonetheless entered into relationship with human beings, beginning in the Bible with God's covenant with Abraham in the book of Genesis:

> When Abram was ninety-nine years old, the LORD appeared to Abram, and said to him, "I am God Almighty; walk before me, and be blameless. And I will make my covenant between me and you, and will make you exceedingly numerous." Then Abram fell on his face; and God said to him, "As for me, this is my covenant with you: You shall be the ancestor of a multitude of nations. No longer shall your name be Abram, but your name shall be Abraham; for I have made you the ancestor of a multitude of nations. I will make you exceedingly fruitful; and I will make nations of you, and kings shall come from you. I will establish my covenant between me and you, and your offspring after you throughout their generations, for an everlasting covenant, to be God to you and to your offspring after you. And I will give to you, and to your offspring after you, the land where you are now an alien, all the land of Canaan, for a perpetual holding; and I will be their God." (Gen. 17:1–8)

It is this God who also seeks to transform us, changing us as he changed Abram to Abraham. As giver of life, this God created all things and is continuously making us as well: This God is transforming the speaker in "Yahweh" from an alienated and unclean misfit to something pure, fit, full of praise, loving, just. This God makes it possible, as in "New Year's Day," always to begin again. This God created "the world in green and blue" in "Beautiful Day," will touch and teach the singer, leading him into new beauty where "all the colours [come] out." This is the God of creation invoked in "Miracle Drug," a song about the power of faith and the miraculous possibilities inherent in God's creation: "God I need your help tonight. . . . I hear your voice / It's whispering / In science and in medicine."

And it is this God without whom we do not exist.

Because of God, we are.

The lyrics of "All Because of You" from *How to Dismantle an Atomic Bomb* suggest a number of possible meanings (don't most U2 songs?), but I read a reference to this God of creation, the Great "I AM"—"All because of you / I am"—since the narrative of the song is about a person who, like the speaker in "Yahweh," is moved from confusion and brokenness to wholeness, who is formed by and exists for God. We can see the creative power of God in one who "heard me in my tune / When I just heard confusion." The psalmist wrote

> O LORD, you have searched me and known me.
> You know when I sit down and when I rise up;
>   you discern my thoughts from far away.
> You search out my path and my lying down,
>   and are acquainted with all my ways.
> Even before a word is on my tongue,
>   O LORD, you know it completely.
>
> (Ps. 139:1–4)

This God, who knows us better than we know ourselves, who can see what we are capable of becoming when we have no idea, who can see the cracks and make us perfect again, is the God of creation, of infinite generative power. This God "created order out of chaos, cosmos out of chaos, and God can do so always, can do so now—in our personal lives and in our lives as nations," as Desmond Tutu writes.[16]

Other Images of God the Father

U2 can also introduce us to another aspect of God the Father: He is a God who is the ultimate source of justice and mercy as well as the God of creation and transformation. As Bono told those listening at the National Prayer Breakfast,

> Look, whatever thoughts you have about God, who He is or if He exists, most will agree that if there is a God, He has a special place for the poor. In fact, the poor are where God lives. Check Judaism. Check Islam. Check pretty much anyone. I mean, God may well be with us in our mansions on the hill. . . . I hope so. He may well be with us as in all manner of controversial stuff . . . maybe, maybe not. . . . But the one thing we can all agree, all faiths and ideologies, is that God is with the vulnerable and poor.[17]

This understanding of God is known as God's "preferential option." Brueggemann explains that since God is both a relational God and a caring God, he "is in solidarity with the most vulnerable and the most needy in society."[18] (That is, this God, who loves us all, loves particularly the disadvantaged who have no other hope). Tutu, the former archbishop of South Africa and a hero of the apartheid era there, often uses the story of the exodus from Egypt (how God, through Moses, liberated his people from slavery), to explain this preferential option: "This God did not just talk—He acted. He showed himself to be a doing God. Perhaps we might add another point about God—He takes sides. He is not a neutral God. He took the side of the slaves, the oppressed, the victims. He is still the same today. He sides with the poor, the hungry, the oppressed and the victims of injustice."[19]

The poor, hungry, and oppressed naturally like to believe in this image of God. But it is becoming more and more mainstream even among the affluent, the well-fed, and the powerful—American Christians. Roman Catholics and many mainstream Protestants have long believed that God cares about social justice. More recently, evangelical leaders like Rick Warren, progressive evangelicals like Jim Wallis and Brian McLaren, and even influential American evangelical groups are likewise expressing their understanding of God as a God of the poor and downtrodden. In the past few years the National Association of Evangelicals has published "For the Health of the Nation: An Evangelical Call to Civic

Responsibility," a report explaining why evangelicals should add poverty and "creation care" to their agendas, and endorsed "An Evangelical Declaration Against Torture."[20] These are acknowledgments from Christians of all sorts that the Scriptures indicate God's passion for all of creation, including those people and things incapable of protecting themselves.

This broadened understanding of God's identity as a God of justice, of course, should lead to action; as Rowan Williams noted, our growing theological understanding of God's identity should shape our lives. We'll talk more about how understanding God as a God of justice and mercy has played out in the music and work of U2 in chapter 3. But what other understandings of God the Father can we discern with the help of U2?

Well, certainly U2 could help us speak of the God of beauty, from whom all beauty comes, and to whom all beauty points. Although the U2 history informs us that initially the members of the band weren't, shall we say, the most proficient musicians in their field, there are powerful and beautiful moments from the beginning of U2's recording career. One of those is "I Will Follow." The band has played the song thousands of times—it continues to be a staple of their live set. But when you listen to "I Will Follow" performed on the "Elevation" tour in 2001 in Boston, site of one of their first important American shows back in December 1980, it remains a thing of beauty. During the bridge, when The Edge's chiming guitar turns the arena into a cathedral, Bono marks it, vamping around and between the ringing harmonics: "Ring those bells. Make those bells ring, Edge. . . . Boston, lift me up on your shoulder. Let's get to a place we could never get over . . . Paradise. . . . Ring those bells. Those bells never gonna get old."

On one level Bono was talking about The Paradise, a club they'd rocked twenty years earlier on their first American tour. But on another, he was remarking on the experience, which you can still participate in to some degree by just listening to the performance. As is often the case at a U2 show, the experience takes the band and the audience out of themselves, lifts them out of this reality where their feet are firmly rooted on the ground and deposits them—for a few minutes, at least—in another place.

Words like "transcendence" are often used for this sort of experience, the ineffable and untellable sort of mountaintop experience we may also associate with religious or sexual ecstasy, with any experience so beautiful or mystical that we are taken out of ourselves and brought closer to the divine. ("Beautiful Day" is both about—and an example of—this kind of experience.)

In U2 songs like "I Will Follow," "Gloria," and "Rejoice," where Bono's melody is often laid over the eccentric workings of The Edge's chords or single notes, we find a substantial amount of musical tension. When we listen to "Gloria," for example, the song is a continuing battle of sorts, between tension and resolution. In the verses, it seems as though there will be no way for these dissonant tones to resolve into any sort of beauty—and yet at the end of each verse, that resolution somehow miraculously happens: "But only in you I'm complete: Gloria." In the long instrumental break, The Edge's solo continues to build tension, Adam's bass solo flirts then chords, and after a dissonant set of guitar chords like clashing cymbals, the final "Gloria—*In te domine*."

It is glorious, a musical healing of a broken universe, and the words here—"Glory to God," parallel what is happening in the music. What was broken is restored, more beautiful than ever; what was unfinished is resolved. This tension and resolution pattern in the music is a theological marvel, for it also explains our understanding of how God has worked—and continues to work—in our world. Begbie, the musician and theologian we mentioned earlier, argues that "the theme of delay is . . . very common in scripture—there is a sense among the writers that things are being in some manner held back . . . 'How long, O Lord?' is not just the wail of the psalmist [or of Bono] but the howl of God's people." Music, he says, can be theologically instructive, because more than any other art form, it teaches us not to rush past "struggles, clashes, and fractures" on the way to beauty, joy, and fulfillment. But beauty, joy, and fulfillment are what music generally hands us, in the end—all of which point us to the God who is their ultimate source.[21]

Theologians might speak then about we call *sacramental theology*, for certainly one of the analogies we might make here has to do with the breaking of and reconstitution of the body of Christ, the tension between what is broken and what becomes whole. Perhaps more importantly, though, sacramental theology speaks of the ability of the things of this physical reality to mediate the things of the transcendent God. While there has been substantial disagreement between Christian traditions about what exactly happens in the Eucharist to the bread and wine (as there are substantial disagreements about many of the theological matters we'll discuss in this book), almost all agree that whether we view them as remembrance of Jesus's own Last Supper, as symbol, as spiritual food, or as the actual body and blood of Christ, there's definite power in that act. In the Scriptures, Jesus commanded his followers to remember and reenact that last supper, that offering of his body and blood in the guise of bread and wine.

In my tradition, the consecrated bread and wine are not considered to be physically changed into the body and blood of Jesus as they are in the Roman tradition, but like all the sacraments, they are physical agents that convey the grace of God to those who participate in them. On their own, they are only bread and wine, just as Larry Mullen observed of U2's music that it has little or no holy power of its own—but in both cases, when God walks through the room (when God gets involved, in the language of *Pulp Fiction*), that physical food, those notes, drum beats, and guitar chords are charged with power to change those who consume them.

Sacramental theology suggests that the physical world has always been the vehicle for our experience of God. As Begbie puts it, "Brought forth from God's own free love, the cosmos as a whole is value-laden, the object of God's unswerving faithfulness and the theatre of God's loving intentions. As such it is able to sing God's praises despite the pollution that evil has brought. God, we said, has pledged himself to the world in physicality—a pledge confirmed in the coming of Jesus, the Word made material flesh."[22]

Incarnation: The Son

"The Word made material flesh": this is incarnation, God becoming human. Bono (in ways that sound very much like Augustine's arguments in his "On the Trinity") argues "that God, if there is a force of Love and Logic in the universe . . . would seek to explain itself. . . . It's pure logic. Essence has to manifest itself. It's inevitable. Love has to become an action or something concrete. It would have to happen. There must be an incarnation. Love must be made flesh."[23]

So it is that the God of creation, grace, and beauty leads us naturally to the second person of the Trinity, Jesus, the Son of God. In response to all the theological confusion that seems to rise around God's identity, on God's sometimes troubling behavior in the Hebrew Testament, and any muddles about what God stands for in the abstract, Jesus becomes an object lesson for us embodied in human flesh. As the theologian Karl Barth wrote, "God is not known and is not knowable except in Jesus Christ."[24]

Bono thus rightly holds up the life and teachings of Jesus as the most valuable guide for Christians about who and what God is:

My understanding of the Scriptures has been made simple by the person of Christ. Christ teaches that God is love. What does that mean? What it means for me: a study of the life of Christ. Love here describes itself as a child born in straw poverty, the most vulnerable situation of all . . . I don't let my religion get too complicated. . . . God is love, and . . . in allowing myself to be transformed by that love and acting in that love, that's my religion. Where things get complicated for me, is when I try to live this love.[25]

The love Bono is talking about is the love described in "Pride (In the Name of Love)," a sacrificial and vulnerable love that seems light-years away from the power and the glory of God the Father (if not from the divine love leading to incarnation). "Pride" is a song about Christ ("One man betrayed with a kiss") and Christ figures, those who are willing to risk all in the name of love. In this song we can see Bono's thoughts about God and love made manifest, just as we can in the band's *Rattle & Hum* recording with blues legend B. B. King, "When Love Comes to Town."

In that song, we are introduced to a speaker (or speakers) who is a certain sort of person—hardened, closed off, faithless, even one who was present at (and thus implicated in guilt for) the crucifixion:

I was there when they crucified my Lord.
I held the scabbard when the soldier drew his sword.
I threw the dice when they pierced his side.
But I've seen love conquer the great divide.

The Christian belief is that the love of God, as manifested in and through the life of Jesus, can conquer any divide. But how is that possible? How can you go from being one sort of person to another? Author Annie Lamott talks about her own conversion experience to Christianity by noting that she used to be over *there* and now she's over *here*—and that there is no earthly way to get from *there* to *here*. But the apostle Paul wrote that Christianity—that is, the world made sense through love and discipleship in Jesus, the Son—might make absolutely no sense to the rest of the world, although in the paradoxes he describes, somehow God's love has made a way for us:

> God chose what is foolish in the world to shame the wise; God chose what is weak in the world to shame the strong; God chose what is low and despised in the world, things that are not, to reduce to nothing things that are, so that no one might boast in the presence of God. He is the source of your life in Christ Jesus, who became for us wisdom from God, and righteousness and sanctification and redemption, in order that, as it is written, "Let the one who boasts, boast in the Lord." (1 Cor. 1:27–31)

Jesus replies to a question about his own teaching paradoxes that "'what is impossible for mortals is possible for God'" (Luke 18:27). This is also, as Bono suggests, the role of Jesus for us, to make manifest the impossible truth about God and God's love through his tangible incarnation as a human being. One of the most challenging and yet galvanizing theological ideas in Christianity is that Jesus was both human and divine, and that his human life on earth was lived as a finger pointing back to the Father who sent him. The writer of the Gospel of John says, "No one has ever seen God. It is God the only Son, who is close to the Father's heart, who has made him known" (John 1:18), and later in John, Jesus tells the leaders of the Jews that "the works that the

Father has given me to complete, the very works that I am doing, testify on my behalf that the Father has sent me" (John 5:36). As I've written elsewhere in words that mirror Bono's earlier theological statement, "Jesus represents our best chance in the biblical narrative to understand God's desires and actions in the form of a human story, which is the only form we can readily apprehend."[26] Origen called Jesus the "*Autobasileia*," or "Kingdom in Person," and his point was likewise that by seeing what Jesus did, we can know who God is.

And by seeing what Jesus did, we should also know what to do.

Since this Person of the Trinity, willing to risk all in the name of love, is embodied in human form, Jesus is a figure with whom we can more readily identify, and he is the member of the Godhead on whom we often find U2 calling. In "Silver and Gold" (from *Rattle & Hum*), the singer pleads, "Jesus, say something!"; in "Peace on Earth," the request becomes "Jesus, could you take the time / To throw a drowning man a line"; in "Wake Up, Dead Man," The Edge and Bono wrote lyrics in which the singer begs Jesus to be present and for his story to be true:

> Jesus, Jesus help me.
> I'm alone in this world,
> And a fucked-up world it is too.
>
> Tell me, tell me the story,
> The one about eternity
> And the way it's all gonna be . . .
>
> Your father, He made the world in seven;
> He's in charge of heaven.
> Will you put a word in for me?

This speaker imagines God the Father as distant, as removed from his own existence here on earth; he may in fact also have his doubts about whether Jesus will answer (he is, after all, talking to a "dead man"), but clearly that hope of reply is all this speaker has in his despair, the only possibility of "order in all of this disorder." Jesus, who has known pain and death, at least represents a better choice for this speaker's prayers—he's more likely to respond than that far off Father in charge of Heaven, although in truth, Jesus is God's response, as Bono told us:

> Essence has to manifest itself. It's inevitable. Love has to become an action or something concrete. . . . There must be an incarnation. Love must be made flesh.[27]

This possibility of order arising from disorder, life from death is of course inherent in the story of Jesus's life, death, and resurrection, present even in dark and contentious moments in the U2 catalog. Perhaps we will still have to ask, "How long will we have to sing this song?" but the answer is that we will sing it only until we can "claim the victory Jesus won / On . . . / Sunday bloody Sunday." As Bono says, though evil and death may have their time, "Finally, in the end, there is light in the world," and this light comes through our understanding of God the Son: Jesus the Christ, the Liberating King.[28]

The Nicene Creed tells us that Jesus is the only Son of the Father, present from the beginning of time, and it relates the central part of his story in this way:

> For our sake he was crucified under Pontius Pilate; he suffered death and was buried. On the third day he rose again in accordance with the Scriptures; he ascended into heaven and is seated on the right hand of the Father. He will come again in glory to judge the living and the dead, and his kingdom will have no end.

Jesus Saves—but How?

This horrible execution by the Roman occupation government—Jesus' willing sacrifice of himself—and his subsequent resurrection by the Father, are, of course, at the heart of Christian understanding. Anselm of Canterbury wrote that Jesus became incarnate as a human being "out of the love and goodness of his Father, for the salvation of us men," and Thomas Aquinas was even more succinct: "We needed God to become flesh if we were to be saved."[29] If you don't believe, literally or figuratively, that Jesus willingly gave himself up to torture and death but was brought back to life, then Jesus is only another teacher, rabbi, or rabble-rouser, however meaningful his words might remain. Still, different Christians have different understandings of how this death on the cross leads to salvation, understandings conditioned by slightly different ideas of God.

A traditional Christian belief about the death of Jesus on the cross is that God the Father required atonement for the wrongdoings and failings of the human race, making Jesus a sacrificial victim who dies on our behalf or pays for our sins in the same way as Jews might have sacrificed a lamb in the temple. With one variance or another, atonement is an orthodox Christian belief, and it seems to be Bono's understanding as well; to the exasperation of his nonreligious friend Michka Assayas, he goes on for page after page in their book-length conversation about his faith, including his understanding of the cross, which he describes as a victory of grace over karma:

> I'd be in big trouble if Karma was going to finally be my judge. I'm holding out that Jesus took my sins onto the Cross. . . . I love the idea of the Sacrificial Lamb. . . . The point of the death of Christ is that Christ took on the sins of the world, so that what we put out did not come back to us, and that our sinful nature does not reap the obvious death.[30]

To the great surprise and shock, perhaps, of many Christians, Bono's general atonement understanding of "the victory Jesus won" on Easter Sunday represents the way that many Christians make sense of the death of Christ: the cross and resurrection represent a victory over sin and death—and over Satan, if one believes in an embodied force of evil and death. The church fathers Athanasius and Augustine spoke of what happened on the cross as substitutionary atonement: Jesus suffered and died so that—for whatever reason—we didn't have to, and in his freely performed act of atonement, Jesus freed us from our obligations or paid a ransom we owed.

As we said, one cannot be a Christian without believing in some way that Jesus' birth, life, and death were necessary parts of God's plan to draw human beings into closer relationship with him.

Atonement is a Christian understanding of how this plan worked that goes back at least to the early centuries of the church and remains official dogma for Roman Catholics, although it is important to note that it is hardly the only way to think of God, Jesus, and the redemption that grew out of Jesus' death. In some Christian understandings, rather than a ransom paid or a substitution, the crucifixion is an example of perfect obedience to God, of a life so attuned to the will of God that Jesus could pray in the Garden of Gethsemane, " 'My Father, if it is possible, let this cup pass from me; yet not what I want but what you want' " (Matt. 26:39b).

The medieval theologian Abelard argued that "we have been justified by the blood of Christ and reconciled to God in this way: through this unique act of grace manifested to us—in that his Son has taken upon himself our nature and persevered therein in teaching us by word and example even unto death—he has more fully bound himself to us by love; with the result that our hearts should be enkindled by such a gift of divine grace, and true charity should not now shrink from enduring anything for him."[31] In Abelard's understanding of death and resurrection, Jesus' example of sacrifice makes us want to likewise draw closer to the God who loves us enough to seek this solution of divine grace.

I also find much to agree with in the argument Brian McLaren advances in *Everything Must Change* about the difference between the traditional atonement idea and the emerging understanding of what Jesus came to do: "Through his life and teaching," McLaren says, "through his suffering, death, and resurrection, he inserted into human history a seed of grace, truth, and hope that can never be defeated."[32] McLaren has also written about how the miracles surrounding the life of Jesus demonstrate the new relationship with and understanding of God that Jesus has come to bring. Although he was not referring specifically to the resurrection, it is, after all the Big One, the sign or wonder that makes everything a new ball game, so I think it's fair to appropriate Brian's argument from *The Secret Message of Jesus* about what it is that these signs and wonders surrounding the life of Jesus are supposed to be telling us to help us understand the crucifixion and resurrection. McLaren suggests the signs and wonders teach us

that God, the good King, is present—working from the inside.
. . . The King is present in the mess and chaos of everyday life
on earth, bringing healing, sight, perception, liberation, wholeness, wholesomeness, movement, health, fullness, nourish-
ment, sanity, and balance. The incursion of the Kingdom of
God has begun.[33]

However one reads the crucifixion and resurrection event, we
can say with the apostle Paul that God sent "Christ Jesus, who
became for us wisdom from God, and righteousness and sanctifi-
cation and redemption" (1 Cor. 1:30). Those last are all economy-
sized theological words, but essentially we can say that the divine
identity of Jesus is bound up in his task to reconcile God and the
human race. Jesus is the redeemer, the liberating king, however it
happened, whatever exactly we may believe about it.

When Love came to town, everything changed.

But U2 sees Jesus as more than just a spiritual redeemer, as
essential as that element of his character is. As Bono notes, Jesus
was a redeemer, but he was also a prophetic figure in the tradition
of Jeremiah, Amos, and Micah, as well as someone worthy of our
emulation: "The Jesus Christ that I believe in was the man who
turned over the tables in the temple and threw the money-changers
out—substitute TV evangelists if you like. There is a radical side
to Christianity that I am attracted to. And I think without a commitment to social justice, it is empty."[34] As we'll discuss in chapter 3, Jesus taught that the kingdom of God (the "reign of God" is
a less sexist way to communicate the same concept, although both
are a little unwieldy) was coming near, that it had been inaugurated
by his teachings, and so his teaching, healing the sick, and feeding
the hungry was embodying God the Father's preferential option. If
God is a God of justice and mercy, then Jesus, who does his father's
bidding, shows us how to *do* justice and mercy—as Bono said earlier, Jesus makes all those years of teachings about God come to
life by living them. So we know what the kingdom of God is about
because we saw what Jesus did; Gustavo Gutiérrez explains it simply: "The reign of God makes the ethical demand that every
believer practice justice."[35]

Ultimately Jesus the Son possesses almost as many attributes as God the Father: He is the Incarnate One, the Lamb of God, the Prince of Peace, the Redeemer of the World, the Defender of the Downtrodden. He is also the bringer of the Spirit, the third person of the Trinity, and it is the Spirit who is involved in bringing peace, comfort, and strength to people of faith after Jesus left this world behind.

Spirit Moves in Mysterious Ways

In many Christian understandings of the Holy Spirit, the third person of the Trinity, there is, as my friend Rowan Williams has phrased it with his characteristic gentleness, "a certain poverty in theological reflection."[36] Christians tend to put either too much emphasis on the Spirit or too little. In charismatic Christian groups like the Shalom community to which members of U2 once belonged, the Spirit is put front and center, and life lived in the Spirit becomes primary (that is, if one is not experiencing gifts of the Spirit, like speaking in tongues or prophecy, one is not considered to be authentically Christian). Steve Stockman reports how Shalom's call for Bono, The Edge, and Larry to leave U2 was actually prompted by a member of the community who claimed to have received a prophecy to that effect.[37] Communities privileging the Spirit often put more emphasis on spiritual gifts than on any other form of revelation.

Other Christians, perhaps in response to this emotional and individual response to the inspiration and the power of the Holy Spirit, recoil from experience of the Spirit or manifestations of the gifts of the Spirit. Think of those denominations sitting in American church buildings who are sometimes referred to—or call themselves—the "frozen chosen"; they may have chosen a less-emotional—and perhaps, inspired—worship and faith practice, but at least they aren't freaked out by people prophesying in ancient Sumerian during their services.

U2, despite their early hurts at the hands of a Spirit-loving community, has engaged the Spirit; Bono often talks about wanting to be where the Spirit is moving (whether in worship, as we will see in the chapter on community, or in the world, as we will see in the chapter on peace and justice), although, since their exit from Shalom, the band has embraced a vision of the Holy Spirit freed from confinement by human institutions. Since *The Unforgettable Fire*, perhaps, we have seen a U2 acknowledging that the Spirit moves in mysterious ways; Irish rock critic Bill Graham wrote of *Unforgettable Fire* that although it was a spiritual album, it was an inclusive one, and if one thought of it as a Christian album, then the Holy Ghost was "the presiding member of the Trinity."[38]

The Holy Spirit is the power of God moving in the world after Jesus returns to the Father (hence Bono's statement "I just go where the life is, you know? Where I feel the Holy Spirit").[39] We find references to the Spirit of God scattered throughout the Bible, beginning at the creation of the world in Genesis: "In the beginning, when God created the heaven and earth, the earth had no form and was empty, and darkness covered the deep, and the spirit/breath/wind of God blew across the waters" (Gen. 1:1, author's translation). This translation helps us to recognize that in the three languages that have been most used to communicate the Bible or to discuss it (Hebrew, Greek, and Latin), "spirit" is the same word as "breath" and "wind"—in each case, the word designates something invisible but powerful, something unseen but life-giving.

So we can speak of Spirit, as some translations of Genesis 1 do, as the "breath of God," or even the "wind of God," blowing across the surface of the deep. Our word "inspire," often used in connection with human acts of creation, comes from the Latin and refers to the idea that something supernatural blows or breathes something into a person that makes that person capable of great things, of experiencing revelation. In speaking of the writing of the Bible, for example, one Christian tradition believes that "the Holy Spirit inspires the writers, but it is the writers who write and speak."[40]

In the writing and recording of the song "One," which has taken on many powerful identities over its history, The Edge says that the inspiration of the Spirit became clearly visible as the song fell together: "At the instant we were recording it, I got a very strong

sense of its power. . . . We were all playing together . . . and everything fell into place. . . . It's the reason you're in a band—when the
spirit descends upon you and you create something truly *affecting*.
'One' is an incredibly moving piece. It hits straight into the heart." [41]

The Holy Spirit moves in our lives, in our work, and in our faith.
Bono said in thinking about "Zooropa" ("And I have no religion /
I don't know what's what"), "There is a line in the New Testament
that says that the spirit moves and no one knows where it comes
from or where it's going. It is like a wind. I have often felt that
about my faith." [42] It's an explanation for his suspicion of institutions that try to cage the Spirit—or insist they have a monopoly on
it. The Spirit moves, and no one knows—or can control—where it
will go. The lines Bono refers to are Jesus speaking of the Spirit in
the Gospel of John,

> "The wind blows where it chooses; and you can hear the sound
> of it, but you do not know where it comes from or where it goes.
> So it is with everyone who is born of the Spirit." (John 3:8)

They might also be referring to "Mysterious Ways," from
Achtung Baby. There are several ways to read "Mysterious Ways,"
as there are with many U2 songs: "It's alright [sic], it's alright, it's
alright / She moves in mysterious ways." On the one hand, there
seem to be references to the story of John the Baptist and the
dancer Salome, who asked for John's head after she had pleased
the king with her dancing. A belly dancer accompanied the song
both on the video for the song and on the "Zoo TV" tour when the
band performed it. But the lyrics also seem to promote the idea of
the Spirit moving in mysterious ways (you can hear The Edge
singing, "Spirit moves in mysterious ways" in the last chorus, in
fact), and when they performed the song on the "Zoo TV" tour, the
band added this, repeated twice:

> Move my spirit, hold me.
> Move my spirit, keep me.
> Move my spirit, take me.
> Move my spirit, teach me.

Bono has said that he likes to think about the Holy Spirit as a
she, and in that tradition, he has plenty of company. Syrian Chris-

tianity identified (and continues to identify) the Spirit as feminine, and certain apocryphal gospels identified the Spirit as female as well, while contemporary theologian Jürgen Moltmann, who has written several well-received books on the Trinity, has said that "the personality of the Holy Spirit can be grasped more precisely with the image of the Mother than with other images."[43]

It's true that the creedal statements of Christianity identify the Spirit as male. The Nicene Creed as spoken in the Western Church, reads,

> We believe in the Holy Spirit, the Lord, the giver of life, who proceeds from the Father (and the Son), who with the Father and the Son is worshiped and glorified, who has spoken through the prophets.

But I too tend to think of the Spirit as feminine, first because linguistically "Spirit" should be translated as feminine, and second, because it makes for a nice theological counterpart to the male images of Father and Son. We all know, of course, that God has no gender, but as we've noted, how we think about God has consequences for our own understanding and belief, and for better or worse (and sometimes it has certainly been for worse), God has been overwhelmingly depicted as male. Jesus, who has many nurturing characteristics, was still most certainly male. Two out of two. But to ignore the nurturing and comforting aspects of God, qualities that are often identified with the feminine, is to ignore important qualities of God—and to undervalue the important work of the Spirit, our divine comforter, inspiration, and advocate.

"Mysterious Ways" can be read in mysterious ways, but one rarely goes badly wrong reading a U2 song in a spiritual way, even if that doesn't represent its entire or only meaning. The verses speak of taking a walk with your sister the moon, of letting her light up your room or space, of letting her talk about things that you don't understand—all of which might be references to the role of the Spirit in the world, which is to enlighten, to fill in the gaps since Jesus left.

In the Gospel of John, Jesus spoke of what the Spirit would do after he was gone, a reality his followers were not yet ready to consider:

"Nevertheless I tell you the truth: it is to your advantage that I go away, for if I do not go away, the Advocate will not come to you; but if I go, I will send him to you. And when he comes, he will prove the world wrong about sin and righteousness and judgment. . . .

". . . When the Spirit of truth comes, he will guide you into all the truth." (John 16:7–8, 13a)

The lyrics of "Mysterious Ways" also talk about someone who doesn't yet see the whole truth but who is enlightened, someone who has been living a half life but who will now see the world in all its beauty:

You've been living underground,
Eating from a can.
You've been running away
From what you don't understand.

Ultimately, "Mysterious Ways" tells a story about someone who is in darkness and is brought into light, who is confused and is brought to understanding. Bono has talked about how one way to read the song is as a song about what happens to a man when he discovers a wise woman, and certainly that's a possible reading. But we can also give the song a theological and spiritual reading: If you'll take a walk with the Spirit, she will guide you into all truth: her light will fill up your room.

Inspired by the Spirit

Bono and other members of the band have talked about the role of the Spirit in their music—the inspiration, being led into truth, the sense of being a part of something much greater than themselves. As a lyricist, for example, Bono in the early days often relied on inspiration at the microphone, as he did in the recording of the song "New Year's Day":

I did five or six verses for the song without writing lyrics, different tracks filled up with different verses . . . they were made up completely on the mike. It was all about speaking in tongues, 'Open my lips, and my mouth shall show forth thy praise.' . . . We were like the Quakers, sitting around until the spirit moved us.[44]

This idea of inspiration has been a part of the band's process all the way to the present. In deciding to put away the tracks that they recorded with über-producer Rick Rubin (who has recorded momentous albums with Johnny Cash, Tom Petty, the Dixie Chicks, and the Red Hot Chili Peppers) for the 2009 album *No Line on the Horizon*, The Edge talked about how those tracks didn't represent the true identity of the band because they lacked the level of spontaneity—of inspiration—that the band has come to rely on and fans have come to love. Rubin's "whole thing is, 'Don't go near the studio until you know exactly what you want to do,' which, of course, is the opposite of how we usually work," The Edge said. But when they began recording again with long-time collaborators Brian Eno and Daniel Lanois, who have learned to make room for the spirit moving, something began to happen: "We went in with Brian and Danny, literally just as an experiment to see what would happen. And suddenly there was this excess of stuff, ideas."[45]

The Spirit moves in mysterious ways.

The Greek word that is translated as "advocate" in the Gospel of John's discussion of the Holy Spirit is *paracletos* or *paraclete*, a single Greek word almost impossible to render into a single word of English. It does contain elements of advocate—one who pleads or intercedes on our behalf—and of counselor, but it also speaks of a comforter—all of these things are part of the Holy Spirit, as we understand her role in the world.

"Grace," from *All That You Can't Leave Behind*, gives us a clear sense of a feminine spirit leading us into knowledge of what is true and beautiful and comforting us with the knowledge that good can come out of bad, beauty out of ugliness. Grace is the name of a girl, as Bono sings, but it is so much more than that. "Grace" is also one of the most important theological words in the Christian understanding—"It's also a thought that changed the world"—explaining how imperfect human beings can be forgiven and accepted by a perfect God. "She carries a pearl in perfect condition," the song tells us; the pearl is often identified with wisdom, something which is said to be given from God, in the Spirit:

> Who has learned your counsel,
> unless you have given wisdom
> and sent your holy spirit from on high?
> (Wis. 9:17)

When we have the Spirit-given opportunity to see the world as God sees the world, with insight and compassion, we can learn to see the things we would traditionally think of as ugly or difficult as beautiful. Just as Bono said of the Christmas story, the beauty and logic of that birth into hardship and vulnerability—well, on the surface it looks pretty dicey. But when we understand it as God does, we can see the beauty and poetry in it, and that is inspiration indeed.

The Spirit is also thought of theologically as the sustainer of life in this universe, particularly for those who accept the classical Christian understanding that God created existence ex nihilo, out of nothing. In this understanding, life—continued life—depends on the Spirit. As Psalm 104 puts it,

> When you take away their breath, they die
> and return to their dust.
> When you send forth your spirit, they are created;
> and you renew the face of the ground.
> (Ps. 104:29b–30)

The Spirit is the life-giving aspect of God, which makes life—which makes us—possible, and we'll close with that recognition again in "All Because of You." Like the singer in "When Love Comes to Town," the singer in "All Because of You" moves from ugliness to beauty, from brokenness to the possibility of healing and wholeness:

> I'm not broke but you can see the cracks
> You can make me perfect again . . .

The final verse speaks of being alive, being born, arriving at the door of the place where we began; of the hope of being able to step back inside where we will be welcomed. Because of God, we are—because of God, there is the possibility of grace, hope, and redemption. In the Spirit, the aspect of God who sustains our lives, our cracks are mended, our lives extended, and our experience of God confirmed.

The notion of the Trinity has bounced many people out of belief, and confounded plenty of others, but I want to close by returning to the idea of Trinity, because it helps us understand both U2 and the church, the subjects of our next chapter. The conception of God as a singularity, one divine subject made up of three different modes of being, has been replaced in the minds of some theologians by God as the "triunity," as Jürgen Moltmann describes it, three persons, one fellowship, which dance together and, in the dance, act together: "Through themselves they form their complete, Trinitarian unity."[46] It's a model of beauty that should appeal to music lovers (and remind us of our earlier Trinitarian discussion of U2 the band), but it's also a model of community that helps us understand how a body of believers—or a body of musicians—do the work to which they are called. If God is a God whose basic identity emerges as and from community, then it makes sense that the people of God would also experience a basic identity that emerges as and from community: Moltmann echoes many thinkers when he says that "the unity of the community is in truth the Trinitarian fellowship of God himself, of which it is a reflection and in which it participates."[47]

Because God is a fellowship of love and action, the church is a fellowship of love and action, because we are alike made in the image of God. And this revelation may, I think teach us a lot about the church—and, if you will follow along with me, a lot about U2 as well.

Chapter Two

Communion

"Sometimes You Can't Make It on Your Own"

Listening File

Before (or while) reading this chapter, listen to these U2 songs. If you have an iPod or other digital music player, you may want to create a playlist or folder containing these songs and set it on repeat.

You can access lyrics for all U2's songs on U2's official Web site: u2.com.

"New Year's Day," *War*
"Two Hearts Beat as One," *War*
"I Still Haven't Found What I'm Looking For," *The Joshua Tree*
"Red Hill Mining Town," *The Joshua Tree*
"Acrobat," *Achtung Baby*
"One," *Achtung Baby*
"Staring at the Sun," *Pop*
"Kite," *All That You Can't Leave Behind*
"When I Look at the World," *All That You Can't Leave Behind*
"Sometimes You Can't Make It on Your Own," *How to Dismantle an Atomic Bomb*

The Quest for Community

On August 21, 2001, Bono's father, Bob Hewson, passed away after a long battle with cancer. It happened in the middle of the

"Elevation" tour, and there was some speculation about what might happen: Would the band go ahead with the shows—including the first mammoth show at Slane Castle in Ireland, just a few days later? Would Bono be up to performing?

Bono and the other members of U2 attended Bob's funeral—The Edge and Larry joined Bono and his brother in carrying the coffin from the church—and at the funeral, Bono sang a new song he'd written for the occasion: "Sometimes You Can't Make It on Your Own."

Bono had gone onstage the night after his father's death in front of 17,000 people at Earl's Court in London, and as he did later at the first Slane Castle show on August 25, he came onstage, knelt, and made the sign of the cross. And there—as, later, at Slane Castle—he was loved by the crowd and his band mates back into something like wholeness, picked up, carried along by a group of people who shared his grief and were willing to walk with him.

At Earl's Court it was 17,000 people—at Slane, it was 80,000. One of them was my friend Zane Wilemon, who was at the first Slane show just after Bob Hewson's funeral. One afternoon a few years ago over beers at the Seminary of the Southwest, Zane told me about the show, where with the typical Wilemon luck, he had found himself down right in front of the stage so that he had an amazing view of everything that happened:

After "Elevation" [the first song], Bono fell to his knees, cried out "Jesus!" threw off his shades, eyes full of tears as he watched the sky. It was obvious where he was. He had buried his father just hours before, and we were all joining him in what became a ceremony of mourning through the celebration of life. All night, Bono referred to his father, the pain, the life, the death, and the far deeper presence of life that was now haunting us all. The honesty and heart-wrenching transparency that Bono poured out that night elevated us all through music and our shared humanity to a place beyond a concert and deeper than church.

Zane was talking about how the crowd picked Bono up—figuratively, of course—and carried him through that night, how they gave back to him a little of what he and the band had given them over the years.

It was an amazing and archetypal evening spent in holy community.

As Adam said of that concert at Slane, "In a situation like that, it's not really about words; you just do the best you can and give your friend as much support as possible."[1] To be with one another—and to be sharing that experience with other sympathetic souls, even if we are rarely so privileged as to share our grief with 80,000 people willing to weep with us—is something we all need, even if we don't acknowledge the value of a church community. But it is one of the things that a church community (or *ecclesia*) can offer when it is doing the work to which it is called, although sometimes, tragically and ironically, churches can leave us feeling more alone, more hurt, more distant from our Creator, than when we encountered them.

Growing up in Ireland as they did, U2 has often talked about how the formal religion they were exposed to—both Catholic and Protestant branches—seemed to be failing the most basic tests of what Christianity should be. "In Ireland," Bono said, "we get just enough religion to inoculate you against it. They force-feed you religion to the point where you throw up. It's power. It's about control. . . . This has nothing to do with liberation."[2]

Since their negative experiences with organized religion thirty and more years ago, the Christian members of the band have been understandably leery of committing themselves to a church again—or of allowing a church or tradition to claim them. Many people have wondered, as we've mentioned several times, if they are actually Christian. Still, they continue to seek God, with even Adam, long the outsider in religious affairs, recognizing that U2's mission is to mingle rock, politics, and spirituality. In a 2001 interview, he noted that while he continues to "have difficulty with the way [spirituality] can be portrayed sometimes," he also believes what Bono had said about the "Elevation" tour: that God was in the house. "I don't quite know what it is . . . but I definitely know when it's there. It doesn't happen every night, but some nights there's a sense of community and fellowship. And people have said there's a spiritual aspect to what's happening in the house."[3]

Brian McLaren is one of many who has recognized this spiritual aspect of U2's concerts: some years ago, he wrote a widely circulated piece on how Christian song leaders could learn something about worship music from U2, and how the group "conducts praise and worship services for 25,000 people all the while creating a commercial and culturally viable perch from which [they] can model a compelling vision of a social gospel."[4]

Bono has, at times, been very clear in stating his rejection of organized religion, saying some years ago that it is "in demise, and I personally won't miss it. I don't think religion has anything to do with God anymore or very rarely has."[5] These comments may be hyperbolic, intended to engender some discussion or even controversy; they may also be, in Bono's mind, dead-on. Perhaps no one who hasn't watched Catholics and Protestants literally try to kill each other, as in Ireland, should get to judge the band's feelings about organized religion. But the result of these negative comments—and U2 has made many similar comments over the years about the church, about TV evangelists, and about the institutions of Christianity—has been that some who are invested in these institutions have taken offense. Sometimes those in the church have suggested that since Christianity is meant to be lived out in community and Bono and the band are no longer part of a formal community, then they must not actually be Christians.

Some have taken the lines from "Acrobat" about belonging to a church—or "The Church"—as an accurate reflection of Bono's take on religion:

> And I'd join the movement
> If there was one I could believe in.
> Yeah, I'd break bread and wine
> If there was a church I could receive in.
> 'Cause I need it now.

It's a mistake to assume that U2's songs of the nineties are necessarily meant to be heard as transparent expressions of the band's feelings; many of the songs are ironic and satiric. But "Acrobat" does reflect a belief that many people have today, particularly younger people. As new longitudinal studies from the Barna Group point out, plenty of people believe that there is no place for them in the church, at least as judged from their own understandings of organized religion. As many as one-third of young adults (with around age forty being a demographic cutoff) consider themselves outsiders to Christianity. The proportion increases to two-fifths of those between sixteen and twenty-nine, and seems to have a generational correlation; that is, each generation is increasingly disaffected with Christianity as they have experienced it. These folks, in general, don't think that the primary brand of Christianity they have seen witnessed on television and in the lives of Christians they meet is a movement they can believe in or a church they can receive in; the vast majority think that "Christians no longer represent what Jesus had in mind, that Christianity in our society is not what it was meant to be."[6] So, in a very real sense, the narrator of "Acrobat" and the members of the band are only reflecting what many in society already think—that the church of the Religious Right, of warfare between Irish Catholics and Protestants, or of Christian intolerance toward other faiths or toward those who believe or act differently cannot command their allegiance.

Perhaps it's no wonder that U2 has been criticized by offended Christians for failing to embrace the full possibilities of Christian community. *Christianity Today* called Bono's theology "light on ecclesiology" (*ecclesiology* is the theology of the nature and structure of the church, from that Greek word *ecclesia*); more judgmental things have been said by others in print and on the Web. Some in the church, however, are not taken aback by the band's rejection of organized Christianity. Archbishop of Canterbury Rowan Williams, who gave a recent speech in which (as you'd guess) he affirmed the importance of the church, actually responds to Bono's oft-spoken criticisms of organized religion with some sympathy:

> If we ask why exactly the religious is so unattractive in the eyes of many, including so many iconic and opinion-forming figures, the answers are not too difficult to work out. Bono's remarks provide an obvious starting-point. Religion is a matter of the collective mentality, with all that this implies about having to take responsibility for corporately-held teaching and discipline;

so religious allegiance can be seen as making over some aspect of myself to others in ways that may compromise both my liberty and my integrity. It may be seen as committing myself to practices that mean little to me, or subjecting myself to codes of conduct that don't connect at all convincingly with my sense of who I am or what is creative and lifegiving for me. It may mean being obliged to profess belief in certain propositions that appear arbitrary and unconnected with the business of human flourishing.[7]

Religion, especially in community, requires the giving up of some autonomy, the acceptance of shared norms. When you have been hurt by a faith community—as U2 were, as I was, as almost everyone is if they remain in one long enough—it can be hard to imagine ever trusting a community enough to want to return to faithful practice with one. For U2, it was an impediment that they have not yet overcome. After Shalom, The Edge went on to say that "I suppose I am a Christian, but I am not a religious person," and Larry, to say, "I am a Christian and not ashamed of that . . . [but] I have more in common with somebody who doesn't believe at all than I do with most Christians. I don't mind saying that."[8]

Since plenty of people cannot conceive of how they might connect (or reconnect) with the church as they have come to understand it, the judgment "light on ecclesiology" might not seem like a particularly damning phrase to apply to U2. Who, they ask, would want to be heavy on ecclesiology? But when church (as a gathering of believers, not as a building) is of paramount importance for your understanding of faith, as is true for most Christians, it turns out to be something very important. Steve Stockman, in his book on the spirituality of U2, said that one of the burning questions he would want to ask Bono would be "How have you kept the vitality of your Christian faith so vibrant in the world of rock music and in the absence of regular Christian fellowship?"[9] And in 2003, when Bono was appearing in churches across the United States to talk about AIDS, debt, and trade in Africa, *Christianity Today*, evangelical Christianity's most important publication, published an editorial that asked how Bono's commitment to Christianity could possibly be carried on outside of the church.

Christianity Today granted that "God may very well be using Bono to challenge the conscience of American evangelicals. It is well within God's frequently evident sense of humor to use a brash rock star in the causes of justice and mercy. If that is so, we hope that God also uses this time to draw Bono into a deeper sense of what it means to be a Christian."[10] It was a clear questioning, if not of Bono's faith, then of its practice.

The central question for some Christians where U2 and Christianity are concerned, then, is this: How can Bono (or The Edge, or Larry) call himself a Christian when he is not part of an established church, since *ecclesia* is how we have always identified other Christians and practiced our faith?

From the beginning of Christian practice—even before many of the new gatherings of Jesus followers had separated from the Jewish synagogues in which many of them began—there was a clear sense that people who believed that Jesus was the Messiah, God's anointed one, were to join together with other believers to worship and work and to pursue together the teachings that Jesus had left behind. And although some evangelical Christians may have an exaggerated sense of how important individual salvation might be, they still tend to gather together in small or large groups to worship and support one another in the faith.

So, on the one hand, perhaps the editors of *Christianity Today* were right to call into question whether Bono understands what it means to be a Christian without belonging to an *ecclesia*, a gathering of Jesus followers. On the other hand, I propose that U2 might be thought of as a sort of *ecclesia*, a gathering of believers who support one another, who do good works as Jesus taught, and who, whenever they go out on tour, actually create an experience that—for many who join them—feels a great deal like worship. McLaren described the "worship" component many people have felt in relation to U2's performances, but his description of the qualities of many emerging Christian communities might also help us recognize those qualities in the band: these new *ecclesias* are virile, courageous, nurturing communities that center their theology on Jesus' revolutionary message of the kingdom and their lives on living out that radical message, and they are communities of spiritual formation whose transformed members seek social transformation.[11]

If we do envision *ecclesia* as a group of people rather than a building, then I think we can make a powerful case for U2 as a faithful community and, in the process, can explore some important ideas about why and how we are saved in community with others once we have begun to come to belief in God.

Could it be that the spiritual and life journey we hear about in "I Still Haven't Found What I'm Looking For" represents a useful early understanding of this concept of community or *ecclesia*? Some would say no. Many Christians have argued that the song clearly proves that U2 are not Christians, or they would know that they've found what they were looking for. So the lyrics have often been taken to be a yearning for something that hasn't been found yet, for a faith or a hope or an understanding that has so far eluded the singer, even though he says he believes:

> You broke the bonds
> And you loosed the chains;
> Carried the cross of my shame.

The video made for "I Still Haven't Found What I'm Looking For," shot on the streets of Las Vegas, can explain things for us beautifully. It begins with a shot of Bono alone, singing the opening lines. He then starts walking—the rest of the video represents a journey of inexorable forward motion to that insistent beat like amplified footsteps—and the other members of the band fall into line behind him. It's true that Bono is still singing these same lyrics—but now he's singing them in the company of others, the people he meets along the way, and with Adam, The Edge, and Larry, his companions on the journey. On the choruses, we can hear the harmony singing of "I still haven't found what I'm looking for," but now we also see the other members of the band—even Adam, who does not sing—"singing" along. (Toward the end, perhaps fed up with the silliness of this lip-synching, Adam walks out of the frame and gets in a cab, but he's pretty good-natured about the whole thing; he raises a beer in salute as he departs.)

Maybe Bono has not found what he was looking for (and many

of us would argue that—even for the faithful—the journey doesn't end with the beginning of faith, so we should all still be looking). But as we see in this video, it is no longer a solitary journey, but one in which people join in, sing along, walk alongside us, even dance—badly—and clap along. When you are no longer alone in seeking—when you are accompanied by others—we see what the church can be, what it is in the lives of many who profess to believe that Jesus carried the cross of their shame.

It can be the place where we gain the strength to journey, and the comfort of having others alongside us. We need to know, in the words of *Pop*'s "Staring at the Sun" that we are "not the only ones staring at the sun"—or to step away from that song's irony, to know that there are others who do not want to go blind, but who want to see.

Even if we have faith, we need others.

We Need Each Other

Archbishop Desmond Tutu often speaks about an African concept called *ubuntu*. Recently, at the National Cathedral in Washington DC, he explained the concept to the dean of the cathedral, Samuel Lloyd, and an audience gathered in the cathedral's nave. *Ubuntu* means, Tutu explained, that "a person is a person through other persons. It is not, 'I think, therefore I am.' It is rather, 'I am human because I belong. I participate. I share.'" What Lloyd concluded from this discussion was that *ubuntu* was actually the most basic element of Christian practice: "We need each other. I can't be me without you. That is the heart of what Christians mean by being the body of Christ, the church."[12]

In this chapter we will explore the music and lives of U2 to see how they seem to call for something more than just individual experience; we will see how the individual members of U2 gave themselves to one another and to the project of the band, as well as how particular songs encourage us to recognize that we need one another. And in the process, we'll engage the theological ideas that explain why it is we need *ecclesia*, even in a world of virtual reality, iPods, and gated communities.

Why should we need others, particularly when our culture often tells us we only need ourselves?

One of the most important stories about U2 is that all of them came into the band broken in some way, missing some pieces that the world deemed necessary to get by. As strange as it seems in talking about the members of, arguably, the biggest rock band in history, a recent article on the band notes, "Each member of U2 is a little of an outsider."[13] There were and have been different reasons for that: early on, Bono and Larry lost their beloved mothers; Bono and Adam were both in trouble in school, with Adam actually booted out for his nonconformist attitudes; The Edge was a Welsh boy who sounded different and was small for his age, sometimes overlooked. Like Adam, he was not born Irish, yet family circumstances had plopped them both down in Dublin. But in the community of U2 they found others who would accept them as they were—and with whom they could be their best selves, with whom they could realize their dreams. As Larry said in an early interview, "The thing that has kept us going . . . is the fact that we are friends. The whole band is based on our friendship."[14]

All of the band members still talk about how the experience of meeting each other changed them—and how their communion is still central to who they are. Adam, who has wrestled with finding his place in the band, with addiction, and with the exclusivity of the Christian faith once practiced by the other three band members, says that what has carried him through the hard times wasn't the wealth, fame, or possessions that come with musical success: "It was the music and companionship."[15] Although generally regarded to be the least "religious" of the band members, it's clear that he recognizes the power of community that formed around U2 and what it has given him, a "survival mechanism," since, as he notes, "We are not hugely intimate with each other, yet there is tremendous tolerance, room and understanding and love."[16]

The Edge seconds that idea of community, remarking,

We have been together all our adult lives, which demonstrates an incredible level of commitment and solidarity between four people who decided to form a band in 1975. All of the reasons why it was a great idea at the time still hold true. On our day we can still make great music together, come up with original ideas and perform emotional, exciting, spiritual shows bursting with the possibility that anything might happen. . . . It is something far greater than any of us could achieve on our own.[17]

Community is an important concept in many spiritual traditions, but it is absolutely essential to any understanding of Christianity. First, as we've seen in our discussion of the Trinity, Christians worship a God who we understand to be in community, ever giving love and returning it, and that understanding of the God in whose image we are said to be made teaches us that fellowship is our rightful place as well. Jürgen Moltmann argues that the triune God represents an archetype of community and fellowship and offers "the model for a just and livable community in the world of nature and human beings." So, indeed, Moltmann can say that the faith community "is the 'lived out' Trinity. In the community, that mutual love is practiced which corresponds to the eternal love of the Trinity."[18] We are called to form loving communities oriented toward God because we are made in the image of a God formed in loving community.

Although all the Gospels (and the second half of the Gospel of Luke that we call the Acts of the Apostles) describe the formation of a spiritual community around the life and teachings of Jesus, the Gospel of John puts in bold print the importance of love for one another: "I give you a new commandment, that you love one another. Just as I have loved you, you also should love one another. By this everyone will know that you are my disciples, if you have love for one another" (John 13:34–35). It's important enough to the writer of John that he has Jesus repeat himself later:

"This is my commandment, that you love one another as I have loved you. No one has greater love than this, to lay down one's life for one's friends. You are my friends if you do what I command you. I do not call you servants any longer, because the servant does not know what the master is doing; but I have called you friends, because I have made known to you everything that I have heard from my Father." (John 15:12–15)

And in case somehow we have missed it (and sometimes I fear we have), just a few verses later Jesus repeats again the only com-

mandment he offers in the Gospel of John: "This is my commandment, that you love one another as I have loved you" (John 15:17).
The Greek word translated here for "love" is *agapē*, a word very
different from most of our cultural understandings of love. When
Adam and the others speak about love in connection with the other
members of U2, they clearly are not talking about romantic or
erotic love, and while they may be speaking about the love we
experience in friendship, the way they describe the transformative
and affirming power of that love also suggests that they are talking
about *agapē*, the sort of love Martin Luther King Jr. defined as
Christian love that was "understanding and creative, redemptive
goodwill for all men."[19]

It also seems to be the kind of love that Bono is ultimately
singing about in "One":

> Love is the temple;
> Love, the higher law.

It is in direct opposition to the selfish and probably eros-centered
love he talks about in *Pop*'s "Do You Feel Loved" and *Zooropa*'s
"Babyface," songs about egocentric desire that leads to pain
instead of people sharing one life with one another, becoming sis-
ters and brothers. Although some stories indicate "One" was originally written as a love song, I've suggested that U2's love songs
are almost never only about two people; they generally have a
larger meaning as well, and "One" has taken on many such meanings, becoming a song about solidarity with AIDS victims and, on
the "Vertigo" tour, a song about eliminating poverty. "One" tells
us that *agapē* love can create a community in which its members
are not the same—but they carry each other (and the phrase is
repeated for emphasis—in case we missed it):

> One love, one blood, one life; you got to do what you should.
> One life with each other: sisters, brothers.
> One life, but we're not the same.
> We get to carry each other, carry each other.

The apostle Paul's notion of the body of Christ seems to be a particularly good match for the idea of community we see emerging

from U2's life and lyrics. The Epistle to the Romans sets out the idea of dying to the world's demands on us and becoming part of a spiritual community, the body of Christ, to which each of us brings different gifts, each of them vitally important. Paul writes, "For as in one body we have many members, and not all the members have the same function, so we, who are many, are one body in Christ, and individually we are members one of another. We have gifts that differ according to the grace given to us" (Rom. 12:4–6).

One of us might be a bassist; one of us might be a singer. But both of us are needed to make beautiful music.

It's a theme Paul returns to in the First Letter to the Corinthians, in which he argues that a community that shares in the body of Christ is one body (the eucharistic prayer, quoting Paul, says, "We who are many are one body, for we all share the one bread"). No matter what our differences, whether "Jews or Greeks, slaves or free," we can be bound together in the body of Christ. Certainly the members of U2 were—and are—different in many ways. Even Larry, Bono, and The Edge, who pursued Christianity ardently, are different in personality, gifts, and passions. The Edge, widely acknowledged to be the musical genius of the band, talked about the process of songwriting and production on *How to Dismantle an Atomic Bomb*, and in doing so, revealed how completely the band relies on the gifts and passions of each member of the body:

> It starts with me, early on. Then when we started to record tracks, it's Adam and Larry that have to step up to the plate. And when it comes to the end, when it's about vocals and finishing the lyrics, Bono is in the hot seat.
>
> My job is to come up with material that will get everyone else excited and inspired. And some of the things I come up with go nowhere. They don't get anyone going. Others take off, and pretty soon, everyone is involved in developing them, and they become U2 songs. Until everyone gets a chance to do their thing with them, they are not U2 songs.[20]

Songs from the whole range of U2's history return to the idea of how much we need one another, how we are completed by one another. "New Year's Day" has been interpreted in many ways, but to hear the lines

And we can break through
Though torn in two
We can be one.

is to reflect on the possibility of community even in the midst of conflict or distress. The title of "Two Hearts Beat as One," also from *War*, points to its status as a U2 love song, but it also points beyond it to the possibility of communion raised in "New Year's Day." And one of the lesser-known songs on *Joshua Tree*, "Red Hill Mining Town," circles around the line "You're all that's left to hold on to," a powerful affirmation of the gift of community in times that are hard for those still holding on in a broken-down mining town. Even as the lights go down on Red Hill, even if love has seen its better day, at least there is still someone to hold on to, and that is something.

Not all communities justify our faith in them, of course. Sometimes we don't become as one; sometimes all we have left to hold onto can fail us. U2's spiritual journey offers substantial proof of this, and many of you—like me—have been hurt by churches or institutions we trusted. U2's Irish roots, of course, offer a cautionary tale about community. The centuries of violence between Roman Catholics and Protestants have engendered in many Irish a deep cynicism about Christianity. In concert, Bono has often carried a white flag, intended to symbolize not just peace, but an avoidance of the extremes. As he told *Mother Jones*, "That's why I used those white flags: this idea of a flag drained of all color, the idea of surrender. If there was any flag worth flying, that was it."[21] This desire to avoid the polar extremes of Irish religion may also account for U2's spiritual choices, which tended to be first for membership in more loose-knit groups not affiliated with formal institutions, and then, after their painful time with a nondenominational charismatic group, for no membership at all. But, since the beginning, they have been seeking community.

The Edge remembered that before they joined any formal Christian community, before there was even much of a band to call a band, their spiritual search had actually created a community called the Monday Night Group that began by meeting in a house, and later grew so large that they had to gather in a meeting room (much like many house churches today, that begin as small informal gatherings). "There was no hierarchy whatsoever, no rules or regulations. Open to all comers, no doctrines, just a group of kids taking an interest in spiritual matters, trying to figure out the big questions." This spiritual group also fed the developing relationships in their band, leading to "deep bonds of friendship and respect between us" that have never diminished.[22]

Later, up to and through the making of the first two U2 albums, Larry, The Edge, and Bono sought out the Shalom community. Though they later would leave Shalom, Bono talks about how important the group was in reawakening something within him, The Edge, and Larry: "They were living on the street, living like first-century Christians. They believed in miracles as a daily business, and they lived the life of faith."[23] He found them fascinating, although their pentecostal fervor also made him a little uncomfortable. He sometimes wondered if they were insane. But—at first, at least—they welcomed the three and made them feel part of the group.

Bono has said that you know if people truly love you if you can be yourself with them.[24] While the three were much drawn to the simple and faithful living espoused by Shalom, the community did not—or would not—honor the passion they had for making music. Shalom could not fathom how being in a rock band could be reconciled with a Christian lifestyle (and certainly it rarely has been), and, Larry remembers, they constantly pushed the three to give up U2 and "do something more spiritually edifying."[25] Christians are counseled to be in the world, not of it, and rock music certainly seemed of the world to their friends in Shalom—I mean, look at Jerry Lee Lewis; look at Elvis; look at the Sex Pistols.

Rock 'n' roll was the devil's music, the music of sex and drugs, rebellion and anarchy.

How could Christians play it?

Among themselves, the three likewise worried that their passion for the music might be standing in the way of their commitment to God. If that was true, of course, Shalom's members were right. Jesus said, in the Gospel of Matthew,

"If any want to become my followers, let them deny themselves
and take up their cross and follow me. For those who want to
save their life will lose it, and those who lose their life for my
sake will find it. For what will it profit them if they gain the
whole world but forfeit their life? Or what will they give in
return for their life?" (Matt. 16:24–26)

And while Jesus did indeed say this, and self-sacrifice is at the
heart of Christian life, Bono has said of that time that

> it was like we were being torn in two. We felt almost subcon-
> scious pressure being applied to us by a lot of people we looked
> up to within that spiritual community that we were in and out
> of. In the end, I realized it was bullshit, that what these people
> were getting close to with this idea was denial, rather than will-
> ful surrender. It was denial, which is the next-door neighbor to
> self-flagellation.[26]

The Edge had a particularly difficult time during this conflict.
At last, he announced that he wanted to leave the band just before
the *October* tour. It was a tough time for all of them, their manager
Paul McGuiness included: he had already engaged a touring crew,
signed contracts for a number of concert dates, made commitments
on their behalf, and lamented to the band that "if God had something to say about this tour he should have raised his hand a little
earlier."[27]

As they thought and prayed about the demands that Shalom
was putting on them, The Edge, Larry, and Bono gradually came
to understand that the loving community that had initially welcomed them into fellowship had become judgmental, and, judging by Bono's standard of love, the people of Shalom were not
allowing them to be who they truly were. As last they decided
that, in The Edge's words, U2 was not your run-of-the-mill hedo-
nistic rock band, that they had found something unique in the
community the four of them had formed together, "and it was
completely bogus to suggest that you couldn't have a legitimate
spiritual life *and* be in the rock 'n' roll business."[28] It was a difficult time, but it led them to valuable insight—the four of them
were a community; they were called to something special; and all

of them could trust that calling. These were spiritual lessons worth holding onto.

People could feel the sense of community in the small clubs they began playing in. Later, as the band got bigger and bigger, they adapted their show and their performances to arena and stadium-sized audiences—and discovered that rather than losing all they had brought to club-sized venues, they were actually creating larger but equally connected communities. Bono says this idea of expanding community came from seeing Bruce Springsteen play a big show: "We went to see him in an arena, and he changed our life. He really communicated. For the first time, U2 realized that a bigger venue doesn't have to dilute the power of our music. We realized it could add to the experience: a bigger crowd, a bigger electrical charge."[29] And those who have been in an arena-sized crowd at one of U2's shows, or who have seen filmed performances like *PopMart: Live from Mexico City* or *U23D*, would affirm that in these shows they have taken their sense of community and written it large.

Most important, in the months after the 9/11 attacks, U2 seemed to be the hub of a worldwide community made up of shocked and battered souls seeking hope and wholeness. When U2 performed at the Super Bowl halftime show in January 2002 (held, ironically, in the Louisiana Superdome, a place they would return after Hurricane Katrina destroyed much of New Orleans), they seemed to be crafting a web of solidarity that encompassed the entire globe. As they played "MLK" and "Where the Streets Have No Name," the names of the 9/11 victims scrolled behind the band, allowing us all to acknowledge and grieve those losses. When Bono opened his leather jacket to display the American flag-patterned lining (yes, the very same Bono who had always renounced flags because he said they divided people), he was, paradoxically, calling for everyone—those in the auditorium and those watching all around the world—to join together. It was said by many people of good will around the world in the early days just after 9/11 that we were all Americans, a powerful statement that they were willing to share our suffering, help us bear our pain, and support us until we were able again to walk on. But Bono and the band made that care and community tangible, carried it on tour, sent it out over the radio. Clearly community—on a small scale, within the group, and on this epic scale, between the band and its audience around the world—is central to understanding U2 and their mission.

Living in Community

The band has weathered hard times and disagreement and stayed together. But why? Why hasn't Bono ever gone out solo (or The Edge, or any of the others, for that matter)? Perhaps part of it has to do with the way the band came together. Adam described it this way: "When somebody said 'Let's form a band,' we thought of it as something to do with people we wanted to be with," and certainly the band has continued to love and be in fellowship with one another for the past thirty years. The Edge said, "When things get really hairy, you start to think, 'Well maybe I should just excuse myself and wander into something a little less hectic.' Then I start to think, 'Well, what would I like to do?' Well, I'd like to play guitar still. . . . 'And what sort of people would I like to work with?' Well, there are these other three guys that I've been getting on with really well for a while."[30] So why leave?

In the band, the members of U2 are with "people we wanted to be with," as Adam put it. They chose to be together, formed deep friendships with those they went onstage with each night, and certainly have created music that will be loved and remembered even after they are gone. But a band is more than a group of people who love each other and work together—just as the *ecclesia* is more than a group of people consciously formed and "getting on really well" with one another. At times, of course, those in U2 have been severely disappointed with—or homicidally angry at—one or more of the members.

When Larry, The Edge, and Bono were considering leaving the band for Shalom in the early 1980s, Adam and manager Paul McGuiness were on the outside, watching with concern and, I would guess, some chagrin. Although The Edge has said, "During the early days, when the rest of us were at the height of our Christian fervour,

Adam was actually the most Christian in his tolerance and his humanity," it's hard to imagine that even a friend who loved and supported you might not also think you were dead wrong.[31]

After the Live Aid show where Bono left the stage to crowd-dive during "Bad" and had been gone so long the band didn't have time to play its hit "Pride (In the Name of Love)," they were furious with him. It was the biggest show they had ever played, seen by people all over the world, and they thought they had lost their one great chance at fame. "We all thought he had completely blown it," Paul McGuiness said. "I think it is fair to say there was a bit of a row afterwards."[32] Bono even imagined leaving the band—until everyone realized that audiences watching on television around the world had been mesmerized by the passion that led him into the crowd in the first place, and their truncated performance had been one of the hits of the show.

Then there was the night in 1993 in Sydney, Australia, on the Zoo TV tour, at the first of two shows that was going to be filmed for a concert video, when Adam was so drunk he missed the show entirely and his bass tech had to go on for him. Afterwards, as Larry reported, "There was a lot of sympathy but we were very clear about what we needed him to do. . . . Some harsh words were spoken."[33] You can't be a band if you can't rely on each other, and showing up for performances is the very least you have to accomplish. The show must go on.

And then there are all the barbs and arrows that inevitably come out of working together for thirty years, arguing about music and political action and plenty of other things. It was never easy in the early days, and it hasn't gotten any easier. Daniel Lanois, producer of the band's most recent album, *No Line on the Horizon*, said that a video clip of Lanois and the band in the studio that had been posted on U2.com might have been any of the "thousands of exasperated moments" they've faced in the recording of even this new album.[34] As all of the members of U2 have said, doing the work that they are called to do is difficult, and often contentious.

One of the truths that has to be acknowledged about community is what U2 confirms for us: When people are drawn to work together, to worship together, to live in community, there will always be conflicts. Jesus knew this even when he was alive—he looked around at the people following him, the crowd trailing him when he spoke, the inner circle fighting among themselves—and he actually gave guidelines for how the community growing up around him ought to function. In the Gospel of John, as we have seen, those instructions centered around love, which is certainly good advice: *Love each other as I have loved you. You must love because you serve a God who is love.*

But love doesn't always solve hard problems; as you may know, you can love someone and still face insuperable difficulties in living or working with that person. Love is a necessary spiritual exercise, but it requires some earthly backup.

That's why it's fortunate that in Matthew 18 Jesus reveals himself to be a down-to-earth leader as well as a lofty spiritual guide. Here we find Jesus giving practical instruction into how the new fellowship might function. He begs his followers not to be stumbling blocks to others in the community, especially those who are like children in their simple faith (the Greek *skandalon* in this passage means, literally, a trap or snare that people might step in, although here it refers specifically to something that causes others to sin). He tells them how to deal with hurts that threaten the community: Go and try to resolve the conflict one on one, gently, if possible. If not, then muster the resources of the community behind you. Only in this way is reconciliation possible:

"If another member of the church sins against you, go and point out the fault when the two of you are alone. If the member listens to you, you have regained that one. But if you are not listened to, take one or two others along with you, so that every word may be confirmed by the evidence of two or three witnesses. If the member refuses to listen to them, tell it to the church; and if the offender refuses to listen even to the church, let such a one be to you as a Gentile and a tax collector. (Matt. 18:15–17)

This method of dealing with conflict strikes some as calling for the complete expulsion of the offending members; N. T. Wright suggests that what the final phrase calls for is treating the person who refuses to be reconciled to the community as an outcast.[35] But I want to suggest—and the example of U2's work at reconciling disagreement perhaps seconds this—that the idea of the "outcast" needs to be interpreted with some generosity. The band has often talked about how every member of the band has to agree to a song—which has led to plenty of discussion and disagreement over the years. Larry describes how that reconciling process worked in the early going on *How to Dismantle an Atomic Bomb*:

> Edge was in the studio doing a lot of work on his guitars. Bono was doing his political work, writing lyrics, coming in and out. At some stage—I think it was towards last Christmas—Bono and Edge said, "We've put down lots of guitars and vocals. Let's have a listen." I said, "I don't think it's as good as it could be." And they said, "If we release this now, we can get on and make another record."
>
> I felt uncomfortable with that. And it was hard saying it. Edge was in the studio for days and nights, working hard, with his screwdriver out, doing these guitar parts. Then I come in, and I'm like, "I'm not sure." It was hard to say it, and it was hard for him to bite his lip and accept that. But that's what makes us U2.[36]

Even honest disagreement can be difficult. Perhaps this is why Jesus spent so much time counseling love—when people are working together in love and fellowship, disagreements seem less divisive. So perhaps this passage from Matthew about how we are supposed to treat those who don't come around at first is not as punitive as it might sound. I don't think this separation always has to mean being tossed into outer darkness, where there is wailing and gnashing of teeth; although perhaps there are some hurts to the community that are so great that there is no chance that a member can ever be readmitted: those sins ought to be great indeed. Many problems—even problems that seem to bring a group to the brink of dissolution—may be resolved, given time and ongoing love and respect. Perhaps it is in this light that Jesus continuously exhorts members of the community to forgive, telling a story in the same part of the Gospel of Matthew about a shepherd who (rather foolishly, in practical terms) leaves behind his entire flock to search for and lovingly return a sheep that has wandered off, and answering the apostle Peter's questions about how many times he should forgive—seven times?—by saying "seventy-seven" or "seventy times seven" (Matt.18:12–14, 21–22 NRSV, KJV).

Effectively, Jesus says that you should forgive those in your community who hurt you over and over again—forever, if you have to—and U2's history gives us examples of that forgiveness at work. Bono tells a story about one show in Newhaven in the early eighties when the band wasn't getting along, and he counted 1-2-3-4, they didn't start the song, and then The Edge almost knocked him out: "Everything had gone horribly wrong with the band fighting, rather than the audience. I threw the drum kit into the audience . . . and Edge hit [me] with a right hook."[37]

That was a hard night—but it didn't break up the fellowship. They forgave each other, and they went on.

Likewise, when Adam missed the show in Sydney, some might have judged him and his substance abuse problem, but the members of the band knew that they could not say anything to Adam that would be worse than the way he was already judging himself for letting them down. As Bono said, "Our first thoughts were for him: 'How are we going to get him through this?' He had bitten off more than he could chew, and it bit him back." But Larry added that along with the sympathy they felt for him, there had to be accountability as well: "We are a band and we need each other. It wasn't going to be possible to continue like this."[38] Forgiveness is something we are supposed to do, but those we forgive should also be working so that we don't have to constantly be forgiving them. The band forgave Adam for missing the show and for messing up his life—and he has since become the one who looks after his brothers. He didn't need to be forgiven again—at least, for that particular offense, and they have journeyed on, dealing with the disagreements and disappointments that have continued to come.

Many people have found strength and hope for their own journeys in "Sometimes You Can't Make It On Your Own," the song that Bono initially wrote about his father. It's a song about relationship, about accepting that we don't have to do everything by ourselves. Even when communities disagree, there can still be love and support:

> We fight all the time,
> You and I . . . that's alright.
> We're the same soul.
> I don't need . . . I don't need to hear you say
> That if we weren't so alike
> You'd like me a whole lot more.
>
> Listen to me now.
> I need to let you know
> You don't have to go it alone.

Like "Drowning Man"—a song written directly to Adam during another time when Bono feared he might be sinking—this song represents what ecclesia does at its best, and what U2 did when Adam fell short. Instead of judgment or exclusion, they were like a church to Adam: they supported him, loved him, gave him their strength to add to his own, and called him to a higher standard. And, in return, Adam transformed his life—which is what is supposed to happen when we have an authentic encounter with the sacred, especially as it is embodied in a community.

So the members of the *ecclesia* are called to things by Jesus himself, things that we can see represented in U2 and their long work and association: they are called to love; they are called to call each other to higher standards; and they are called to work for the good not just of the group, but for the world. In the way U2 has often approached these requirements, we see how the church functions at its best: as a community of love, responsibility, and justice.

Love One Another

It can be hard to quantify love between professional entertainers; we all know of show biz families or rock bands who have hated each other's guts offstage, yet onstage have put on an act of togetherness for the fans. And, of course, there are bands—just as there are families and churches—who don't pretend to be able to get along. The Police, for example, never pretended to be best friends, and on their 2008 reunion tour, they rocked on stage while hating each other off it. During their final show, Sting actually announced from the stage, "The real triumph of this tour is that we haven't strangled each other. That doesn't mean it hadn't crossed my mind —or Andy's or Stewart's."[39]

And as understandable as that can be—we all have lived in families, worked in offices, or been in churches where it was difficult to get along—we also know that we are called to something higher, something supremely difficult—but also something supremely beautiful that we know best in the community of those we love and trust. Perhaps Bruce Springsteen captured this higher calling in his eulogy for E-Street Band keyboard player Danny Federici:

> Let's go back to the days of miracles. Pete Townshend said, "a rock and roll band is a crazy thing. You meet some people when you're a kid and unlike any other occupation in the whole world, you're stuck with them your whole life no matter who they are or what crazy things they do."
>
> If we didn't play together, the E Street Band at this point would probably not know one another. We wouldn't be in this room together. But we do. . . . We do play together. And every night at 8 p.m., we walk out on stage together and that, my friends, is a place where miracles occur . . . old and new miracles. And those you are with, in the presence of miracles, you never forget.[40]

When Jesus called the members of the *ecclesia* to love each other, he was not saying, "Agree with each other." But he was saying, "These are your people; together, you will walk the path, and you need to learn to get along, at least." In the desert tradition, Amma (Mother) Syncletica spoke about the damage that is done to both individuals and faith communities when people are constantly packing up and moving on. How can you learn to be yourself in Christ unless you spend concentrated time in a community of people who are also trying to learn that? she asks. It's too easy to pick up and move anytime you feel uncomfortable or misunderstood. Stick for awhile. Walk on together. And maybe something miraculous will emerge from your fellowship.

We have seen how U2 have accepted that fact, have recognized that they can only be completely themselves in the band. As Bono says, "I thank God on a daily basis for my life in U2, because not only did this job put my talents to use, it put my insecurities and weaknesses to use. That's the miracle for me."[41]

But miracles do not come easy. When Jesus was calling for love, he was actually calling us to other things as well; he called for companionship, he called for understanding, and he called for sacrifice. He showed us, from his own example, how we should be prepared to sacrifice everything for each other. Again, from the Gospel of John:

> "This is my commandment: love one another, as I have loved you.
>   No one can have greater love than to lay down his life for his friends." John 15:12–13 NJB

That's the kind of love we see described in "Pride (In the Name of Love)":

> In the name of love,
> What more in the name of love?

It reminds me of one of my very favorite stories about U2. During the 1980s, the band had campaigned for a national holiday to recognize Dr. Martin Luther King Jr., and many Americans did not respond well to their advocacy. In Arizona, particularly, there was a lot of angry talk, and even some death threats. One was very specific, and the police and FBI took it seriously. *Don't play Arizona,* this threat said. *And if you do, don't play "Pride (In the Name of Love)," because I will blow Bono's head off.*

Although this was a credible threat, the band did not want to be intimidated. They went ahead with the show. Bono tried to put out of his head that someone had threatened to shoot him, and when it was time to perform "Pride (In the Name of Love)" Bono remembers,

> I just closed my eyes and I sang this middle verse, with my eyes closed, trying to concentrate and forget about this ugliness and just keep close to the beauty that's suggested in the song. I looked up, at the end of that verse, and Adam was standing in

front of me. It was one of those moments where you know what
it means to be in a band.[42]

If you have seen U2 perform, you know that normally Adam is
over to stage left, playing steadily; to imagine him actually moving across to center stage and in front of Bono to shield him from
possible attack as he sang is to see Jesus's words—"No one can
have greater love than to lay down his life for his friends"—and
U2's words—"What more in the name of love?" come to life.

Adam was willing to risk his life for his friend, both because he
loved him and because he believed in what they were doing
together. Bono was risking his life to sing their song about love and
justice; could Adam do any less?

We are all called to love. Likewise, we are called to lift each
other up, to make it possible for everyone around us to be their best
selves, remembering the South African concept of *ubuntu*. The
idea that "I cannot be who I am meant to be without other persons"
speaks to the question of identity, but it also speaks to our formation. Desmond Tutu has written, "None of us comes into the world
fully formed. We would not know how to think, or walk, or speak,
or behave as human beings unless we learned it from other human
beings."[43] In an *ecclesia* we are formed—as ethical people, as people of faith—by one another, and we are called to the highest standards of behavior by one another.

Stanley Hauerwas argues that this is, in fact, the great task of the
church: "to be nothing less than a community capable of forming
people with virtues sufficient to witness to God's truth in the
world."[44] The song "When I Look at the World" teaches us about
how we need each other to see what we cannot see alone:

> So I try to be like you;
> Try to feel it like you do.
> But without you it's no use;
> I can't see what you see
> When I look at the world.

And then, by the end of the song, we see the formation taking place.
The singer says that he can't wait—the time has come to step up to
the plate, to live up to the challenge of seeing. One person, at

least—this character—is transformed because of the challenge and support of community—which is what *ecclesia* is supposed to do.

In U2's life and work, they often talk about how being a member of this band calls forth their best work, their highest aspirations. No song is accepted for the album until everyone is convinced it is as good as it can be, and the band is constantly pushing one another to give the best concerts, to conceive the best tours. As Bono says, "I don't want to betray the trust of our audience—but more than that, the gift, and the life that comes with that gift. When I feel we're abusing that, when we're just knocking them out, treading the boards . . . I don't think this band would be capable of doing that."[45] The stories that emerged from the recording sessions for *No Line on the Horizon* suggest that the band still refuses to settle for anything less than the best, freshest, most powerful music they can make together.

The word communion is often used in the church as another word for the sacrament of the Eucharist, the shared meal of thanksgiving in which very different members of the body come together, where as the liturgy says,

> We who are many
> Are one Body
> For we all share in the One Bread.

In response to *Christianity Today's* questions about Bono's ecclesiology and his understanding of Christianity's core tenets about community, Beth Maynard wondered

> how a man who talks about how doing the hard work of staying with Edge, Larry, and Adam in a 25-year friendship (not to mention with his wife Ali in a 20-year marriage) is a "sacrament" could fail to see the same sacramental power in the hard work of relating, for an equally long time, to a specific group of other local believers whom you did not select.[46]

It's a potent thought. And perhaps Bono, at least, is coming back toward a realization that there may be something to this church idea. His speeches in churches to rally support for social justice

come at the same time he has been owning his faith more openly—
witness his sermon at the National Prayer Breakfast—and also recognizing that there may be more to the historical traditions and
manifestations of Christianity than he has sometimes given them
credit for. In a recent book-length interview, Bono actually seems
to be acknowledging the value of the biggest—and most venera-
ble—strand of organized Christianity in response to criticism of
the Pope and the Catholic Church by his secular friend Michka
Assayas:

> Let's not get too hard on the Holy Roman Church here. The
> Church has its problems, but the older I get, the more comfort I
> find there. The physical experience of being in a crowd of
> largely humble people, heads bowed, murmuring prayers, sto-
> ries told in stained-glass windows, the colors of Catholicism—
> purple, mauve, yellow, red—the burning incense . . .[47]

It's a long way from "I'd take bread and wine / If there was a
Church I could receive in," and perhaps, a lesson for many of us. I
too fled far from the church as a result of the same kind of spiritual bullying the Christian members of U2 met in their youth, and
for many years I was one of the "spiritual but not religious" people that Rowan Williams spoke of earlier in this chapter.

But along the way, since I didn't have a band to take me in, I discovered that I needed to be in community with other people who
also believed in the "kingdom come" but who still hadn't found
what they were looking for. Eventually, against my will (Spirit
moves in mysterious ways), my search brought me back to the
church, if to a different form of Christianity than I'd learned growing up. I had insulted and derided the church for decades as hypo-
critical, ineffectual, and ignorant, but what I found when I returned
to a church of people seeking God and the chance to heal the world
were the same things it seems U2 has found in their communion
over the last thirty years: accountability, support, love, strength for
the journey, and an experience of the transcendent.

And in the church, finally, I have also found support for the idea
of justice that has always moved me, just as the members of U2
have supported one another in their work for peace, justice, and

equity in the world. So it's to the relationship between faith and justice—particularly as we understand it with the help of the music and work of U2—that we turn at last.

The ultimate outcome of belief lived out in community should be a changed world.

Chapter Three

Social Justice

"We Need Love and Peace"

Where Should Faith Take Us?

What makes U2 the biggest band in the world—and Bono the world's most-recognizable rock star—does have a little something to do with music, we must admit. There's the string of successful albums and tours, words that have spoken to the hearts and souls of millions of people, videos and concert films that have brought U2 to millions who have never seen them in person. But how does that make U2 any different from any other long-lived and successful rock band? Why do people respond differently to U2 than to, say, the Rolling Stones, or Def Leppard, or Metallica, all bands still successfully making music after decades in the business?

Part of it is the difference in the music, of course. As I've argued throughout the book thus far, U2's music is attempting to do more than chronicle sexual conquests and incite rebellion, rock 'n' roll's traditional subject matter. It is not about partying hard or driving fast, two other traditional subjects. And even though it is about living life to the fullest, its conclusions about what the fullest life might be lead us away from hedonism and self-interest and toward concern for others and a deeper connection to something beyond ourselves.

In their music—and in their lives—U2 has told us that there is more to life than what our cultures—or even, sometimes, our faith traditions—may tell us. Life is not about acquisition or conquest—nor is it about just saving yourself for an afterlife, for heaven some day. These are three unhealthy secular and sacred examples of what Brian McLaren calls "framing stories," overarching cultural narratives that shape how we live our lives. McLaren argues that their prevalence in our culture is poisoning us, and you don't have to spend much time thinking to recognize the truth of that.[1]

In writing this book, what I have hoped to suggest is that in their music, lives, and words, U2 offers us a different framing story, something opposed to both the cultural touchstones and to many contemporary Christian understandings. As we've already seen, U2 models for us the idea of spiritual journey, rather than that of reaching a spiritual destination. They teach us about the divine, how God manifests love and mercy in the universe, and how God can be a part of our lives. They show us how we are made for one another, and how we can only become our best and most realized selves in the company of others who love and support and challenge us.

And the logical offshoot of these lessons seems to be this final lesson from U2, the final chapter to their framing story: If we want to live a rich and interesting (not to mention holy) life, they tell us it should be a compassionate and useful life, a life devoted to peace and justice.

We are called to carry each other, not because it is easy, but because it is right, and we are called to elevation, not purely for ourselves, but for one another. In the Christian tradition, as U2 will illustrate for us, a simple focus on otherworldly salvation—what Bono has derided as self-righteousness and self-serving piety—is a misunderstanding of our faith.

We are not simply called to salvation; we are also called to justice. Why? As we'll see, our wisdom traditions—particularly the Hebrew tradition—call for it. Jesus of Nazareth modeled it. The Bible, that collection of narratives, poetry, theology, and law, requires it.

And God, so far as we can understand, wants it.

Or, at least, so says Bono. In his sermon at the National Prayer Breakfast, he told the gathered dignitaries,

> God may well be with us in our mansions on the hill. . . . I hope so. He may well be with us in all manner of controversial stuff . . . maybe, maybe not. But the one thing on which we can all agree, among all faiths and ideologies, is that God is with the vulnerable and the poor. God is in the slums, in the cardboard boxes where the poor play house. God is in the silence of a mother who has infected her child with a virus that will end both their lives. God is in the cries heard under the rubble of war. God is in the debris of wasted opportunity and lives, and God is with us if we are with them.[2]

Powerful words. They have the ring of truth about them. Bono certainly seems to believe them. But can we?

Can these articles of faith become ours as well?

And if they could, what could happen to the world, to our societies, to us?

Let's begin with an audacious chapter toward the end of U2's story. The world's richest human—and, we should note, to be fair, the greatest philanthropist in human history—Bill Gates,

tells a story about a transformational moment involving Bono
that recently opened his eyes to what might be accomplished in
the world:

> A few years ago I was sitting in a bar with Bono, and frankly, I
> thought he was a little nuts. It was late, we'd had a few drinks,
> and Bono was all fired up over a scheme to get companies to
> help tackle global poverty and disease. He kept dialing the pri-
> vate numbers of top executives and thrusting his cell phone at
> me to hear their sleepy yet enthusiastic replies. As crazy as it
> seemed that night, Bono's persistence soon gave birth to the
> (RED) campaign. Today companies like Gap, Hallmark and
> Dell sell (RED)-branded products and donate a portion of their
> profits to fight AIDS. (Microsoft recently signed up too.) It's a
> great thing: the companies make a difference while adding to
> their bottom line, consumers get to show their support for a
> good cause, and—most important—lives are saved. In the past
> year and a half, (RED) has generated $100 million for the
> Global Fund to Fight AIDS, Tuberculosis and Malaria, helping
> put nearly 80,000 people in poor countries on lifesaving drugs
> and helping more than 1.6 million get tested for HIV.[3]

At first glance, let's acknowledge how bizarre this story is: a
rock star networking with a bunch of billionaires in order to help
those who are less fortunate? (Imagine this with Mick Jagger and
Rupert Murdoch, for example, or insert your own celebrity and bil-
lionaire; it could be a party game.) But anyone who has read this
far knows that this incident is true to the story of U2, a story in
which Bono meets with the Pope, presidents and prime ministers,
and capitalists and corporate executives, a story in which the band
plays gigs for Amnesty International and world hunger and pro-
motes the ONE movement. For those of us who have watched
Bono become, in many ways, the most important activist in the
world, working to shift awareness in the West from personal comfort and state security toward debt, AIDS, and trade issues in
Africa, and toward poverty relief worldwide, there's nothing surprising here.

The question is, though, why does he do it?

Is it altruism? Is it guilt? Or is it possible that, as we have been suggesting, U2's pursuit of peace and justice grows out of their desire to be faithful to their beliefs?

I can understand that—although it certainly isn't for me—for some people this is not just a rhetorical question. Christians and other people of faith sometimes seem to be very selective in how they approach social and political issues, with simultaneous compassion for some people and antagonism or indifference toward others. Some Christians staff adoption hotlines but don't seem to notice the babies starving in Africa or India. Some Christians simultaneously oppose abortion but support the death penalty. Some Christians advocated the invasion of Iraq at the same time as they worshiped the Prince of Peace.

And some Christians, following the examples of St. Francis and Mother Teresa and Dorothy Day and Martin Luther King Jr., have devoted their lives to helping "those who have none" (to use my son Chandler's phrase for those who are poor, sick, homeless, hungry, victims of violence and oppression, or otherwise in need).

How is it possible for Christians to come to such different conclusions about what they are called to do? Well, as conservative Bible scholar Scot McKnight acknowledges, all Christians—even those who claim to read the Bible literally and live out every part of it—adopt the sections that seem most relevant to them and adapt them to fit the culture of which they're a part: "We pick and choose."[4]

Knowing this, McKnight argues that the question becomes, What do we pick and choose, and why? How do we faithfully live out the Bible in the twenty-first century? Up to—and perhaps, judging from some state referendums, including—the national election of 2008, abortion and gay marriage seemed to be the social issues that many Christians cared most about—when they cared about social issues at all. What twentieth-century Christianity seems to have bequeathed us, according to my friend Phyllis Tickle, is a "biblically-sanctioned Code of conduct . . . to be believed in as a means of salvation" instead of the redeeming Son of God.[5] Although this seems to be changing (not quickly enough to suit Phyllis or me, I'd guess), many American (and other) Christians still seem to care mostly about their own salvation, as they understand that salvation. Focus on the Family, one of America's most powerful and best-known conservative Christian groups, heads their list of essential "guiding philosophies" with this:

> We believe that the ultimate purpose of life is to know and glorify God and to attain eternal life through Jesus Christ our Lord, beginning within our own families and then reaching out to a suffering humanity that needs to embrace His love and sacrifice.[6]

And few Christians would argue that making God known and glorifying God are at the heart of Christian belief; as we noted, it's what we find U2 doing in "Gloria" and "Rejoice" and "Yahweh," and many other songs, and it is certainly one of the things we should constantly be doing. But is attaining eternal life the "ultimate purpose of life" for "a suffering humanity"?

Bono suggests that it isn't—or, at least, shouldn't be. As he told an interviewer from *Rolling Stone*: "If you are not committed to the poor, what is religion? It's a black hole."[7] To believe in the kingdom come—but not to attempt to do anything to bring it closer—is a spiritual dead end, according to U2.

But for far too many Christians, belief in God seems to lead only to an attempt to make other people believe in God—so that they can make other people believe in God. And all of this belief must be a good thing, somehow, but how does it change those led to belief? And how does it change the God-created world these new believers inhabit?

"Love and Peace or Else," from *How to Dismantle an Atomic Bomb* calls for this change, the *metanoia* we discussed earlier:

> As you enter this life
> I pray you depart
> With a wrinkled face
> And a brand new heart.

Personal transformation matters. But the song also calls for more, for us to lay down our treasure, to lay down our weapons. Why? Because we also need love and peace. And to get there, even the daughters of Zion and sons of Abraham will have to change the way they look at the world. Instead of exalting wealth, power, and

pleasure, those things that seem to rule the secular world—or security, which seems to rule the sacred—we need new values.
We need a brand new heart.

Faith as piety or as evangelism doesn't lift us out of the cycles of violence, out of the circle of poverty. Those who need, still need; those who hate, still hate. The Holy Land, where the daughters of Zion and sons of Abraham have been killing each other for centuries, is just one place where it becomes clear that simply being faithful—that is, having faith in God, as you understand God—isn't enough to change the world. Bono reminds us that our prayer is the prayer we are given by Christ: " 'Thy Kingdom come / Thy will be done on Earth as it is in Heaven.' . . . We've got to start bringing Heaven down to Earth now."[8] So if we imagine God's will being done on Earth, and if we understand God as a God of justice, mercy, and love—and see those qualities represented by Jesus in a life of love, good works, and peace—then can it ever be enough solely to believe in God and to encourage others to believe?

In his recent book on Christian practices, McLaren sums up the spiritual journey in a way that can help us understand the journey we have taken with U2 this far. It's not about individual belief, although that's important; it's about living that belief in community, for the benefit of the world:

> I'm assuming that this whole thing is not about me. I'm assuming that the community of faith doesn't exist for me. I'm assuming that my own contemplative practices aren't ultimately about me. I'm assuming that maturity as a spiritual human being isn't complete unless it sends me out of myself into the faith community. But it's not simply about "us" either—in the sense of our church, denomination, or religion. No, I'm assuming that the faith community isn't complete unless it, in turn, is sent outside of itself into the world with saving love. In other words, I'm assuming that the church exists for the world and not the reverse.[9]

Faith as piety is not sufficient—and faith acted out as love and care for one another within an *ecclesia* is not sufficient, either. If our belief has changed us—and if we are part of a community of people who have been changed—then that change should be reflected not just in ourselves and in our faith communities, but in our world. And it's that understanding—acted on by U2 as it toured for Amnesty International and performed at LiveAid; by Bono when he campaigns for African aid, debt relief, and AIDS drugs; by The Edge when he works for the well-being of musicians in hurricane-ravaged New Orleans—that we want to explore now.

Listening to the Prophets

In the Christian tradition, a faithful attention to social action actually begins with the words of the Hebrew prophets, faithful outsiders who spoke truth to power and uncomfortable words to the comfortable. We sometimes get hung up in the supernatural aspect of prophecy, the idea that the Hebrew prophets could see the future or channel the Almighty; what's more important is that the prophets were people of love and compassion and faith who could also see what needed to be changed in individual lives and in society for God to be truly honored and served. They were people like Jeremiah, who told the religious people of his day that God was fed up with their simultaneous religiosity and cruelty to others:

> Yahweh Sabaoth, the God of Israel, says this: Amend your behaviour and your actions and I will let you stay in this place. Do not put your faith in delusive words, such as: This is Yahweh's sanctuary, Yahweh's sanctuary, Yahweh's sanctuary! But if you really amend your behaviour and your actions, if you really treat one another fairly, if you do not exploit stranger, the orphan and the widow, if you do not shed innocent blood in this place and if you do not follow other gods, to your own ruin, then I shall let you stay in this place, in the country I gave for ever to your ancestors of old. (Jer. 7:3–9 NJB)

The prophet Isaiah, best known to many through the beautiful words and music of Handel's *Messiah*, was also a take-no-prisoners preacher who proclaimed that faithfulness had to be more than just faith and worship, and his message from God too was powerful and painful: that worship was an abomination to God as long as the actions of the worshipers remained unjust:

Trample my courts no more;
bringing offerings is futile;
    incense is an abomination to me.
New moon and sabbath and
    calling of convocation—
I cannot endure solemn
    assemblies with iniquity.
Your new moons and your appointed festivals
    my soul hates;
they have become a burden to me,
    I am weary of bearing them.
When you stretch out your hands,
    I will hide my eyes from you;
even though you make many prayers,
    I will not listen;
    your hands are full of blood.
Wash yourselves; make yourselves clean;
    remove the evil of your doings
    from before my eyes;
cease to do evil,
    learn to do good;
seek justice,
    rescue the oppressed,
defend the orphan,
    plead for the widow. . . .

How the faithful city
    has become a whore!
    She that was full of justice,
righteousness lodged in her—
    but now murderers!
Your silver has become dross,
    your wine is mixed with water.
Your princes are rebels
    and companions of thieves.
Everyone loves a bribe
    and runs after gifts.
They do not defend the orphan,
    and the widow's cause does not come before them.
                    (Isa. 1:12b–17, 21–23)

Just as Jeremiah and Isaiah attacked religiosity and self-serving piety, Bono has often taken on displays of religious fervor without corresponding displays of justice, particularly as evidenced by TV evangelists, a frequent target of the band since *The Joshua Tree* era:

> It broke my heart . . . remember, I was a believer. Though I understood the power of the Scriptures they were quoting from, and I did believe in the healing powers of faith, I was seeing it debased and demeaned. What's always bothered me about the fundamentalists is that they seem preoccupied with the most obvious sins. . . . But I couldn't figure out why the same people were never questioning the deeper, slyer problems of the human spirit like self-righteousness, judgmentalism, institutional greed, corporate greed. . . .
>
> We thought they were trampling all over the most precious thing of all: the concept that God is love. These televangelists, they were the traders inside the temple, that story where Jesus turned over their tables.[10]

Amos, a Hebrew prophet who was often quoted by Martin Luther King, also called to account those who claimed to be followers of God but who didn't perform acts of justice and kindness. Amos heard God saying,

> For I know how many are your transgressions,
>   and how great are your sins—
> you who afflict the righteous, who take a bribe,
>   and push aside the needy in the gate.
> Therefore the prudent will keep silent in such a time;
>   for it is an evil time.
>
> Seek good and not evil,
>   that you may live;
> and so the LORD, the God of hosts, will be with you,
>   just as you have said.
>
> (Amos 5:12–14)

Finally, Micah (and I could cite plenty of other examples, but I think you're seeing how central this issue of faith and action was to the Hebrew prophets who made up a great chunk of the Scriptures Jesus studied and embodied) also asks whether God wants worship or right action. In one of the most succinct faith statements in the Hebrew Bible (we'll shortly look at a similarly concise one from the Christian Testament), Micah says this:

> He has told you, O mortal, what is good;
>> and what does the LORD require of you
> but to do justice, and to love kindness,
>> and to walk humbly with your God?
>>> (Mic. 6:8)

In the Hebrew tradition, as the prophets explain it, faith should lead to justice: God requires both. But the "justice" called for in the Hebrew Testament is not what we normally think of as justice in our culture, the punitive treatment of those who have in some way violated the laws and statutes we have set up. It's a positive behavior, not simply a punishment. If you look up *justice* in *The Oxford Companion to the Bible*, you find this: "Justice. *See* Righteousness." This is how it should be: the same Hebrew word is used for justice and righteousness (*sadiq* or *tzedek*), and it encompasses all of life under God, what we are supposed to do as well as what we are not supposed to do.[11] The Hebrew prophets embrace this idea: What you imagine God wants you not to do is not all important; you are also called to do the right thing, to help those less fortunate, to avoid making their lives any more difficult. Bono understands this. David Heim observed that Bono's sermon confronting the powers that be at the president's prayer breakfast and calling them to do more for the world's poor was "a prophetic moment, or as close to one as official Washington allows."[12]

This comparison of U2 to the Old Testament prophets is not just fanciful. Rock 'n' roll has often spoken prophetic words to society. Just in recent years, Green Day attacked the complacency and complicity of a warmongering, consumerist, and intolerant American society with songs from their album *American Idiot*, and Bruce Springsteen, on *Magic* and other albums, has written powerful and painful songs about war and our willingness to pursue it at all costs. Maybe we can't imagine The Edge, Larry, Adam, and Bono with long beards carrying staves, but in many of their songs,

U2 explicitly calls people, institutions, and nations to task for their failure to love and do justice, to help the poor and friendless, to pursue peace. The band has often asked its native Ireland to do more, to do better, to love peace instead of internal strife.

And it has also done the same for America, which has been like an adopted country for the band. In "Bullet the Blue Sky" from *The Joshua Tree*, for example, the singer speaks prophetic words against America that will sound similar to those we've been hearing from the Old Testament prophets:

> See across the field;
> See the sky ripped open;
> See the rain comin' through the gapin' wound,
> Howlin' the women and children
> Who run into the arms
> Of America.

Larry said that at the time of that album, Bono had a love/hate relationship with America. Bono saw all that was good about America (or could be good about it), but he had also just come back "from El Salvador and The Conspiracy of Hope Tour and seeing the brutal face of US foreign policy."[13] Like Amos, Bono could love a people (America in this case) and say, at the same time, "I know how many are your transgressions, and how great are your sins."

This relationship is a vital part of understanding the prophetic impulse: you have to love something to hate its failings. Why criticize if you don't care? Why call something or someone to something higher if it doesn't really matter to you? The Hebrew prophets were talking to their own people and taking their own institutions to task. Martin Luther King Jr. used to say that the reason he was so disappointed at the failures of the church to work for peace and justice was that he loved it so dearly.[14] So it has been with U2 and America: if they hadn't been fed by its music, loved its landscape, been treated well by its people, it would not matter so much that America has sometimes fallen short of its best ideals, had fought unnecessary wars, had subjected people to poverty and oppression.

Rabbi Joseph Telushkin has observed, "The true prophet is in conflict with his times."[15] The Hebrew prophets called people to something better—to better behavior and a better understanding of what really mattered to God—and that's what U2's songs often do as well. Whether it's violence, or indifference, or greed, U2 has written about it, and often, spoken out against it. The examples run from early in the band's career to the present moment. There's "New Year's Day," for example: "And so we are told this is the golden age / And gold is the reason for the wars we wage." Wealth may be a primary value in contemporary culture but the song calls to account our infatuation with money and material success.

On *The Joshua Tree*, as we have seen, we also find moments where the band is responding to growing interests in doing justice—and calling attention to American failures in that regard. One of the most powerful is "Mothers of the Disappeared," another song drawn from Bono's time in El Salvador. Adam said that Bono was "inspired by this strange, almost silent protest of the mothers of people who had disappeared without any trace but were assumed to be victims of torture and murder. Bono had met with them and understood their cause and really wanted to pay tribute to it."[16] The era of *Los Desaparecidos*—"The Disappeared"—was a horrible time in Latin America. The separate incidences had too much in common to ignore, and they always implicated friends as well as foes. As Bono noted, the terrifying regimes who "disappeared" people were backed by the United States because they were anticommunist, although they stood against many of the democratic values that America claims to champion around the world:

> People would just disappear. If you were part of the opposition, you might find an SUV with the windows blacked out parked outside your house, just to let them know they were watching you. If that didn't stop you, occasionally they would come in and take you and murder you; there would be no trial. The mothers wanted to know where their children were buried. The same had happened in Chile, the exact same thinking to inspire terror and with identical support: The United States of America.[17]

U2 loved the United States, as they proved beyond doubt after 9/11. This nation had given them their biggest breaks, had welcomed them, and was the land of Johnny Cash and B. B. King and Bob Dylan, all of whom opened up new musical vistas for them. All the same, it was clear to them that America needed to be called to a higher standard, its dark and violent undercurrents brought into the light. Prophets are countercultural.

Rolling Stone writer Anthony DeCurtis described how the beauty, cultural richness, spiritual vacancy, and ferocious violence of America were the main subjects of *The Joshua Tree,* and they were explored in many ways: "the title and cover art, the blues and country borrowings evident in the music, the imagery that pervades songs like 'Bullet the Blue Sky,' 'In God's Country,' and 'Exit.'"[18] *The Joshua Tree* is shaped by a love for and fierce anger with America, a desire to call it to account, and that love and anger come through in many ways.

"There was a lot to despise about America back then," Bono said. "And whilst communism turns out to be one of the worst ideas the world ever came up with . . . to support everything that's anti-communist was [also] a really bad idea. . . . They were bad times. I described what I had been through [in El Salvador], what I had seen, some of the stories of people I had met, and I said to Edge, 'Could you put some of that through your amplifier?'"[19]

In "Mothers," in "Bullet the Blue Sky," and even in "In God's Country" ("We need new dreams tonight"), a prophetic voice is condemning—and, at the same time, reminding—America about its highest self, its great calling. "There used to be a tradition in America," The Edge said at the time, "of people in rock & roll holding a mirror up to what was going on around them. Asking awkward questions, pointing out things. I suppose *The Joshua Tree* is in that sort of tradition."[20]

U2's albums and tours of the 1990s illustrate another element of the Hebrew prophetic tradition: the extravagant prophetic gesture, the hyberbolic action. In his introduction to a book of sermons inspired or informed by U2, Eugene Peterson wrote that prophets "confront us with the sovereign presence of God in our lives. If we won't face up, they grab us by the scruff of our necks and shake us into attention. Amos crafted poems, Jeremiah wept sermons, Isaiah alternately rebuked and comforted, Ezekiel did street theater. U2 writes songs and goes on tour, singing them."[21]

As Peterson attests, the prophetic tradition included words as well as actions, and in the prophetic tradition, these latter were often outlandish, over-the-top, intended to get people's attention. He mentions Ezekiel's street theater:

The word of the LORD came to me: Mortal, set your face toward Jerusalem and preach against the sanctuaries; prophesy against the land of Israel and say to the land of Israel, Thus says the LORD: I am coming against you, and will draw my sword out of its sheath, and will cut off from you both righteous and wicked. Because I will cut off from you both righteous and wicked, therefore my sword shall go out of its sheath against all flesh from south to north; and all flesh shall know that I the LORD have drawn my sword out of its sheath; it shall not be sheathed again. Moan therefore, mortal; moan with breaking heart and bitter grief before their eyes. And when they say to you, "Why do you moan?" you shall say, "Because of the news that has come. Every heart will melt and all hands will be feeble, every spirit will faint and all knees will turn to water. See, it comes and it will be fulfilled," says the Lord GOD. (Ezek. 21:1–7)

The words are important—but what makes people listen is the prophet's moaning. It's the hyperbolic action that makes the words come to life.

Similarly, in the book of the Hebrew prophet Hosea, we find this:

Yahweh said to Hosea, 'Go, marry a whore, and get children with a whore; for the country itself has become nothing but a whore by abandoning Yahweh.'

So he went and married Gomer daughter of Diblaim, who conceived and bore him a son. (Hos.: 1:2b–3 NJB)

The marriage relationship—so central, so sacred to many of us—becomes a profane and obscene show that can draw attention to Hosea's central proclamation: that the people of God are no more than unfaithful whores.

The Hebrew prophets weren't afraid to strip naked, act crazy, put on a show. What they did was often wild, crazy, over the top, like, say, dressing up as the devil. Or mounting a ridiculously expensive rock 'n' roll show—a "magical mystery tour for the nineties . . . a blitzkrieg of words and images" that everyone wants to experience—while flashing the words "PANIC," "EMERGENCY," and "EVERYTHING YOU KNOW IS WRONG" at the throng and forcing them to listen to interviews from war-torn Sarajevo.[22]

The horned character of MacPhisto became part of the excess that marked these tours and music. The Edge said of the "ZOOTV" and "Zooropa" tours, "That character was a great device for saying the opposite of what you meant. It made the point so easily and with real humour." Bono, who had to transform into this character, at first rebelled against wearing the horns, but he put them on and realized that the ridiculous action would actually sell whatever he said:

> It was the maddest-looking thing, but it helped, because when you are dressed as the Devil your conversation is immediately loaded, so if you tell somebody you really like what they're doing, you know it's not a compliment. . . . I called the Archbishop of Canterbury and told him that it was great that the Church didn't seem to stand for anything. It was death by cupcake.[23]

The irony and the excess made it impossible for people to turn away; at the same time as U2 was spotlighting our spiritual ennui in songs like "The Playboy Mansion"; our love of consumption, flash, and surfaces in "Miami"; and our lack of faith in "Wake Up, Dead Man." To objections that the band was no longer spiritual, Bono replied that he thought there was still plenty of soul. "I think it shines even brighter amidst the trash and junk," he said.[24]

This use of the spectacular and the theatrical to get and hold people's attention was also something used by Jesus, who was a figure very much in the tradition of those prophets. When he overturned the tables in the temple in Jerusalem, it was a reflection of his indignation and anger—but it was also street theater that got everybody's attention for his messages: *Wake up! The kingdom of God is coming near! The world is going to change—and it needs to. Look at all this!*

Working for the Kingdom

We have heard Bono speaking about his understanding of Jesus, that Jesus represents for us the will of God expressed in its most human way. But what is it that Jesus does? The New Testament scholar and Anglican bishop N. T. Wright says that Jesus inaugurates for us a quest for peace and justice. In his apologetic *Simply Christian*, Wright begins by talking first about justice because, he says,

> It is important to see, and to say, that those who follow Jesus are committed, as he taught us to pray, to God's will being done 'on earth as it is in heaven.' And that means that God's passion for justice must become ours too. When Christians use their belief in Jesus as a way of escaping from that demand and challenge, they are abandoning a central element in their own faith.[25]

For Wright, that central element is what scholars call "the kingdom teachings" of Jesus, which he discussed in parables and acted out in healing and feeding miracles. In this understanding, the kingdom teachings and actions of Jesus are intended to show us how to live. In a recent talk, I heard Wright affirm that it is in the life of the flesh-and-blood Jesus that we best understand God and God's kingdom and assert that Jesus' identity cannot be understood apart from the kingdom teachings. Other scholars would concur. Bruce D. Chilton notes the "clear agreement" among the Gospels of Mark, Matthew, and Luke (the so-called Synoptic Gospels) that the kingdom of God (or heaven, as it is represented in the Gospel of Matthew) is the central theme of Jesus' message, "a primary focus of Jesus' theology."[26]

The kingdom of God/kingdom of heaven seems to have both a present and a future meaning when Jesus talks about it in the Gospels. In the Gospel of Luke, for example, when Jesus casts out demons, he tells people that "the kingdom of God has come to you" (the Greek verb *epthasen* suggests "is here" or "has arrived"). This links Jesus' work of healing with God's kingdom and suggests that, with Jesus, the reign of God has begun. But clearly it has not been concluded; you don't have to look around very hard to see that even though Jesus taught and healed and fed people, even though people of faith today may be trying to act with kindness and compassion, the world is still a mess. The kingdom has, simultaneously, past, present, and future orientations. Although Jesus has begun God's work, and we are to continue it, a time is coming when that work will be complete, when God will truly rule on earth as he does in heaven, when God's tide of peace and justice will roll across the whole planet.

The name for the theological talk about the end of things, the time when we trust that God's reign will come in fullness, is "eschatology," which comes from the Greek words meaning "talk of last things." The problem comes when Christians make their interest in the kingdom of God entirely eschatological, looking only toward the future, toward the next life, with little interest in this one. The coming perfection of the world is an important element of faith, and we do see the impulse toward eschatology in U2 songs like "Still Haven't Found What I'm looking For," "Where the Streets Have No Name," and "The Playboy Mansion" ("Then there will be no time for sorrow / Then there will be no time for shame"). In the world to come, at the time when God perfects all things, then we will find what we're looking for, street names won't matter, and there will be no time for sorrow.

These are beautiful teachings. But when the "then/now" balance of understanding the kingdom teachings is skewed entirely to the future end of the seesaw, we won't act in the present, which is what the kingdom teachings seem to require. In the Gospel of Mark, when Jesus begins his ministry by talking about the kingdom, he links us to it: "Now after John was arrested, Jesus came to Galilee, proclaiming the good news of God, and saying, 'The time is fulfilled, and the kingdom of God has come near; repent, and believe in the good news'" (Mark 1:14–15). That is, we are called to "repentance" (that metanoia or transformation we have been talking about) because the kingdom has come near; Jesus' teaching of the kingdom requires action from us.

U2 seems to exemplify the understanding of the kingdom teachings called "inaugurated eschatology," which is that we are called to work toward the coming of God's reign by doing the things that Jesus began doing when Jesus inaugurated the kingdom of heaven: feeding the hungry, healing the sick, working for peace, preaching a transcendent God who alone is worthy of worship. In one of Steve Stockman's sermons, he preached that the kingdom "has been at the forefront of U2's music and work. . . . And they are not prepared to wait until God puts it all right in heaven. . . . Bono has been crusading across the globe in an attempt to make this kingdom in which he believes so passionately more and more of a reality."[27]

If we believe in the kingdom come, as we said earlier, we are called to action, working in concert with God. "When you decide to be a citizen of the heavenly kingdom," Rowan Williams writes, "what you do and say will become a foretaste of God's kingdom, a sign of what is coming. Your life will give a foretaste of God's rule," and your task will include inviting others to join you in resisting the rule of all those powers working against or undercutting God's desire for peace and justice in the world, all the powers that "seek to keep people in slavery."[28] (Or in the most succinct formulation of this I have found in Williams: "We are to act in such a way that the nature of God becomes visible.")[29]

The kingdom teachings are at the heart of Jesus' ethical and spiritual demands on all who follow him, and this insistence on action is reinforced by stories and actions in the Gospels that are not part of the kingdom teachings. In the Gospel of Luke, for example, we find a story that is found nowhere else in the Bible, the parable of the Good Samaritan. In this story, Jesus expands our conception of who we are supposed to care about by telling a story about a Jew who is left for dead by other Jews but rescued by his people's ancient enemy, a man from Samaria. The parable of the Good Samaritan fits alongside the ethical kingdom teachings in demanding that we help others—and not just those who look like us or believe like us. Our neighbors are any people who require our help, since, they are all, as Martin Luther King Jr. put it, "fellow human beings made from the same basic stuff as we, molded in the same divine image. . . . The good neighbor looks beyond the external accidents and discerns those inner qualities that make all men human and, therefore, brothers."[30]

When the band played "One" on the "Vertigo" tour as recorded in Chicago in 2005, the song's long-standing message that we get to carry one another had expanded well beyond a couple in relationship, or even beyond sufferers of AIDS. As the band played, Bono talked about the ONE campaign, the project "to make poverty history," and spoke about how it was not okay for a child to die because she or he had nothing to eat—even if that child was on the other side of the world. We are all one, the band was saying; the whole world is our neighbor. "People want to be a part of that," Bono said, remembering the tour, "and they feel they are a part of that, part of the generation that can actually turn the supertanker of indifference around."[31]

Throughout the Gospel of Matthew we find the continuous call to action, the condemnation of belief that doesn't show itself in acts of mercy and justice. Those who hear Jesus' teachings but do not do them, we are told, are not true followers of Jesus. In Matthew 25, Jesus summarizes the ethical teachings and the calls to action that fill that Gospel in a way that should remind us of the Hebrew prophetic concerns for all those who suffer:

> "Then the king will say to those at his right hand, 'Come, you that are blessed by my Father, inherit the kingdom prepared for you from the foundation of the world; for I was hungry and you gave me food, I was thirsty and you gave me something to drink, I was a stranger and you welcomed me, I was naked and you gave me clothing, I was sick and you took care of me, I was in prison and you visited me.' Then the righteous will answer him, 'Lord, when was it that we saw you hungry and gave you food, or thirsty and gave you something to drink? And when was it that we saw you a stranger and welcomed you, or naked and gave you clothing? And when was it that we saw you sick or in prison and visited you?' And the king will answer them, 'Truly I tell you, just as you did it to one of the

least of these who are members of my family, you did it to me.'" (Matt. 25:24–40)

The lesson could not be clearer: what Jesus teaches in the Gospels about the kingdom of God and in his storytelling and ethical instruction is a life in which we submit to God and in which we carry each other. What we do in this life and in this world matters. (Or, as Bono says, "I take Christ at his word: 'On Earth as it is in Heaven.'")[32] What Jesus teaches us is a life in which we help those who need help, feed those who are hungry, and pursue justice and peace for all people, here and now. Heaven, if it comes, will be lovely. But people are starving now. (Or, as The Edge says, "Our stance as a band is that we believe in heaven but we live as if we didn't.")[33]

So if Jesus is our model—and N. T. Wright reminds us that "Christians not only inherit the Jewish passion for justice, but claim that Jesus embodied that passion"—then much of the Bible seems to call for us to work for peace and justice.[34] I would contend, in fact (although I don't have the space or inclination to examine the whole Bible here), that the *entire* story of God we find in the Bible asks us to work for peace and justice. Marcus Borg would agree, for he argues that salvation is both personal and social: "The Bible is not about the saving of individuals for heaven, but about a new social and personal reality in the midst of this life"; Scot McKnight supports this understanding of the Bible as well: "If you are doing good works, you are reading the Bible aright. If you are not doing good works, you are not reading the Bible aright;" and Brian McLaren says that the Bible "is the story of the partnership between God and humanity to save and transform all of human society and avert global self-destruction."[35]

So the Hebrew Bible, the teachings of Jesus, and an expansive reading of the entire Bible as a narrative of God's engagement with the world (as opposed to reading it simply as a rulebook or a devotional guide, for example) indicate that God wants us to direct our attention to the world's brokenness. But why should we need to help heal the world if God is all-powerful? Many Christians—particularly those who seem to be waiting for God to set things right—

call on God to fix things. In this recent American presidential election, for example, I heard preachers on TV and radio praying for the election of a particular candidate, and in my life, I have heard plenty of prayers for specific outcomes. In fact, I have myself prayed a prayer or three for something I really wanted—or wanted to avoid.

Doesn't God fix things for the faithful? Why do we need to do anything?

Songs like "If God Will Send His Angels" and "Wake Up Dead Man" imagine God's direct intervention—and seem to take God to task for not cleaning up the mess we have made for ourselves. In "If God Will Send His Angels," the singer is seeking hope and faith and love, but "God's got his phone off the hook" and might not pick up, even if he could. Meanwhile it's become simply impossible to get Jesus' attention since "they put [Him] in show business." It seems to be a failure of both God and religion, one we also see in "Wake Up Dead Man," one of the most corrosive—and truthful—U2 songs of the 1990s.

"Wake Up Dead Man" is a prayer, and more than a prayer—it's a plea that the world make sense. *Is there order in all of this disorder?* the narrator asks Jesus. *Is it like a tape recorder? Can we rewind, get a do-over?* And alongside this plea for understanding, there's the question—*Why aren't you—or God—doing something?* "I know you're looking out for us," the narrator says, but all the same, *I'm alone in this world, and it's a pretty messed-up world.*

The question of why evil exists if God exists and if God is anything like the God we imagine has to be the most potent question about faith. Theologians call it *theodicy,* and people (including me) continue to write books and essays about it, looking for some hard-won wisdom to live our lives by. If God is good, why is there pain and suffering in the world? If God is just, then why do some good people suffer and some bad people thrive? Why doesn't God just wave a magic wand or something and fix everything if he's so good?[36]

Some people lose their faith in God when they discover that God is not a jukebox you can put a coin in and get the tune of your choice; others lose their faith when they discover that God has not intervened to save one of his faithful, despite their faultless life or the horrible nature of their suffering. Since, as I mentioned, you could write a book on theodicy (and I have), let's focus on the most pertinent idea for us as we imagine the music of U2. In the Reformed Jewish *Book of Prayer*, I am told there is a line about the relationship between prayer and action that sounds very much like what we just heard The Edge saying: "We should pray as though it is all up to God, but we should live as though it is all up to us." Theologians who have wrestled with the Bible and with this question have decided that after praying hard, we are to live as if it is all up to us, since, in the words of St. Theresa of Avila, we are the hands of Christ in this world.

If God will send his angels to straighten things out, well and good. But if God doesn't—and clearly, most of the time, given the state of the world, that doesn't happen, and probably it shouldn't—we have to become angels for one another.

God is always at work, Rowan Williams reminds us, "opening the door to the future even when we can see no hope." But God generally works through the processes he has set in motion, processes that include—and rely—on us. "God has," Williams says, "mysteriously—made a world in which what human beings do can help or hinder what he achieves . . . when we give him space, through our prayerful consent to and identification with what he wants, things may happen that were otherwise unpredictable."[37] With our help, that is, God's faithful can help continue God's vision for creation begun by God, announced and furthered by Jesus, and left in our hands, for good or ill.

In "Miracle Drug," from the *Atomic Bomb* album, Bono's lyrics speak of that partnership, of how God continues to move through human actions:

> I hear a voice;
> It's whispering
> In science and in medicine,
> "I was a stranger
> You took me in."

God moves in the world in all that the faithful do (and, I believe, in much that the nonfaithful do; with Bono, I would affirm that "God chooses to work with some pretty poor material," and I include myself in that category, just as Bono did). God can use the work of those who do science and medicine, and politics, and economics, and every other kind of work—to help bring the kingdom of God nearer.[38]

Contemporary Prophets

In the centuries since Jesus modeled a faithful love of God that leads us to faithful service of our neighbors, whoever they are, many people have talked about the necessity of faithful action. For U2, the most important of those voices might be that of Martin Luther King Jr. and the liberation theologians of Latin America.

U2's debt to and admiration for Martin Luther King is obvious, and is expressed in songs like "MLK" and "Pride (In the Name of Love)," but it is also reflected in their insistence that faith and social action must go hand in hand. For King, an ordained minister who was the son and grandson of ministers, an ongoing source of sadness was the failure of the church (or, it must be admitted, parts of the church, particularly parts that were in the American South; Jewish and Christian leaders of Catholic, Protestant, and Orthodox flavors marched with King, but almost all were from the North) to acknowledge and work toward equality and justice.

In one of his sermons, King said these words that by now should sound familiar to us, since Bono has been channeling them for years:

> In spite of the noble affirmations of Christianity, the church has too often lagged in its concern for social justice and too often has been content to mouth pious irrelevancies and sanctimonious trivialities. It has often been so absorbed in a future good 'over yonder' that it forgets to make the gospel of Jesus Christ relevant. . . . Any religion that professes to be concerned with the souls of men and yet is not concerned with the economic and the social conditions that cripple them is the kind the Marxist describes as 'an opiate of the people.'[39]

When Bono wrote the lyrics to "Crumbs from Your Table" for the *Atomic Bomb* album, he also talked about how religion should deal with real-world needs as opposed to "pie in the sky":

> And you speak of signs and wonders,
> But I need something other.
> I would believe if I was able,
> But I'm waiting for the crumbs from your table.

"That line was a shot at the Church," Bono explains, "because I felt at the time that the Church wasn't doing anything about the AIDS emergency."[40] It was acting, in other words, as an opiate rather than an antibiotic, preaching indifference as an anesthetic rather than action as a solution.

King spoke about this failure of the American church to confront real-world problems like poverty and war in one of his most famous and powerful writings, "Letter from a Birmingham Jail." King argued that if the church did not remember its roots and its sacrificial call to serve others, it would "be dismissed as an irrelevant social club."[41] And history, I fear, has borne out his prediction. All over the Western world, people have abandoned the church, and even here in America, young people are leaving the church in ever-greater numbers and not returning. In contrast, the church is growing and vibrant—as King could have predicted—in the Global South, where faith and daily life are inextricably entwined. We will consider some of the lessons growing out of the Global South in a moment, but we should hear King's final and very specific words on how we should marry our spirituality and our work for the world, since they have clearly had a powerful impact on U2.

In what turned out to be his final sermon to his home *ecclesia*, Ebenezer Baptist Church in Atlanta, Georgia, King spoke to his community about what he called the "drum-major instinct," the human desire to be at the front of the parade, to be important and respected, and how that impulse can poison our spiritual lives and our national life if we find ourselves at the front of the wrong parade of values, which we often do. In his final address to his congregation, King spoke words similar to Jesus' words in chapter

25 of Matthew, and summed up a lifetime of teaching and prayer and action. A recording of the sermon was played at his funeral only two months later, and here's how King said he'd like to be remembered:

> I'd like for somebody to mention on that day that Martin Luther King, Jr., tried to give his life serving others. I'd like for somebody to say that day, that Martin Luther King, Jr., tried to love somebody. I want you to say that day, that I tried to be right on the war question. I want you to be able to say that day, that I did try my best to feed the hungry. And I want you to be able to say that day, that I did try, in my life, to clothe those who were naked. I want you to say, on that day, that I did try, in my life, to visit those who were in prison. I want you to say that I tried to love and serve humanity.
>
> Yes, if you want to say that I was a drum major, say that I was a drum major for justice; say that I was a drum major for peace; I was a drum major for righteousness. And all of the other shallow things will not matter.[42]

Remember King's assessment of a faithful life well lived the next time you hear "Pride (In the Name of Love)," and think about what life might be calling you to do:

> Free at last, they took your life;
> They could not take your pride.
>
> In the name of love;
> What more in the name of love.

As Bono said of their song "MLK," the Scriptures "talk about the blood crying from the ground. And with 'MLK,' you have just that, the blood crying from the ground—but not for revenge, for understanding."[43]

U2 seem to have understood. Martin Luther King Jr. taught U2 that what really matters, even if you are a person of faith, is a life of love and service, and in their songs, in their references to King, in his image, flashed during their shows, they have carried his message far and wide.

The other great theological influence on U2 and Bono, particularly, has been Latin American theology, especially the strain called liberation theology, which brings together faith and politics to attempt to help the disenfranchised and the oppressed. Liberation theologians like Gustavo Gutiérrez argue that the separation we have imposed between our faith and the systems we live in is artificial. To speak about a theology of liberation, he writes, "is to seek an answer to the following question: what relation is there between salvation and the historical process of the liberation of man."[44] Moreover, it is to answer that the two are intimately connected. To know God and to seek salvation, Gutierrez argues, is "to do justice."[45]

This is why liberation theology speaks of God's "preferential option" for the poor, and why it calls people to live out (or into) their faith by becoming a "friend of the poor." Liberation theology grows out of our awareness of the choices made by the God who sided with Hebrew slaves against their powerful Egyptian oppressors, by the God who chose to become incarnate as one of the working poor. Clearly this God is with the poor, has a special regard for the poor, as Bono told those gathered at the National Prayer Breakfast.

And Jesus—well, Jesus just makes this preference clear, rejecting the company of the rich and powerful for the despised and lowly, and ultimately showing what happens when a person who wants to do the right thing runs afoul of a corrupt and corrupting system. Christ came, according to Leonardo Boff, to liberate humankind, to show

> that God as well as human persons cannot be imprisoned within preestablished [sic] structures, whether social or religious. . . . With Christ, all is shaken. With him, the old world is finished. And a new one appears, where people have the opportunity to be judged not by what the moral, religious, and cultural conventions determine, but by what—through good sense, love, and total openness to God and others—is discovered as the concrete will of God.[46]

And that concrete will of God, of course, is liberation for all, of their minds, souls, and bodies.

Bono, as you will remember, has been profoundly shaped by travel in Latin America (and throughout the Third World, as it used to be known, or the Two-Thirds World, as it is now some-times called). In the *Rolling Stone* interview in 1987, he was already calling for a marriage of Christian faith and social action, and he was acknowledging the powerful vision of liber-ation theology:

> I am really inspired by it. I was in the Church of St. Mary of the Angels, where liberation theology has a base, in Nicaragua. . . . I attended a mass, and the priest asked all those who had lost a loved one for the revolution, fighting the *contras* or whatever, to stand and come forward and call out the name of your loved one. And all these people stood, and called the names one by one, including sons and daughters. And with each name the congre-gation would cry, "*Presente!*"—meaning they were present. It was amazing to see such solidarity. If you are not committed to the poor, what is religion?[47]

The experience of traveling the world, of being with the sick and the poor and the embattled around the globe, has shown Bono a vision of the world that diverges from the typical Western vision of self and security. For those of us on the upper rungs of the lad-der, in (relatively) safe and stable societies, it is easy to be self-satisfied and to look at the charity we distribute as adequate and appropriate. But Bono, shaped by the lens of liberation theology, demands more than charity from those in power: "I'm interested in charity," he acknowledges. "But I'm much more interested in justice."[48] Liberation theology's "friendship with the poor" has been a powerful motivator for Bono, which is obvious in all of his recent work in Africa. Bono began doing political networking on behalf of the poor in Africa because, he said, they didn't have a National Rifle Association or tobacco industry lobbyists to plead their case in the halls of power:

> I remember feeling angry about how the poor have to come to us in the West with their cap in hand. I thought, God does not see it like that. Whether you're the CEO of a giant corporation or a poor farmer in Africa, God doesn't see any difference. I just thought we should give the poor more respect. . . . I want to have the kind of representation for poor people where they don't have to go up begging for crumbs from our table.[49]

It was up to him, he decided, to become the lobbyist for the poor. Still, it is not just our money being requested, although that is needed; it is also our lives. As Desmond Tutu, also speaking powerfully from the liberation tradition, remarks,

> God calls on us to be his partners to work for a new kind of society where people count; where people matter more than things, more than possessions; where human life is not just respected but positively revered; where people will be secure and not suffer from the fear of hunger, from ignorance, from disease; where there will be more gentleness, more caring, more sharing, more compassion, more laughter, where there is peace and not war.[50]

It is a vision of the kingdom that the Bible—and U2—call us to work toward.

We have said that God is a God of justice, love, and mercy; we have said that we worship and follow this God in groups of like-minded people. We have said that the Hebrew and Christian traditions we find recorded in the Bible call for us to work for social as well as individual salvation. So what do we do to ensure that, with other believers, we act in such a way that (as Rowan Williams put it) the nature of God becomes visible in us, that (as Desmond Tutu put it) we create a new society where all people count?

Here is where U2 has much to teach us. We have already seen how the music of U2 often calls us to work for the betterment of the world, but the actions of the band are equally important in understanding our role in the world. Bono said some years ago in response to what Christians were supposed to be doing, "Well I am not sitting here with flowers in my hair, chanting. . . . I do have responsibilities, and actions speak louder than words."[51] Words are important, and often they can touch others and motivate them to act; Bono has said a lot of words in concert and to world leaders. He has asked U2 fans to care about war and suffering, to commit their voices and their pocketbooks to these causes.

But the ultimate answer to the question of what we are supposed to do about the suffering world is not talk. It is action. As Bono said, music is all well and good: "When you sing, you make people vulnerable to change in their lives. You make yourself vulnerable to change in your life. But in the end, you've got to become the change you want to see in the world."[52] This final charge has been echoed by Christian advocate for peace and justice Jim Wallis, as well as in recent speeches of Barack Obama. Clearly it is an idea whose time has come.

Once we have talked about what we are supposed to do and decide to do it, then we do it together. All of us are called to work for peace and justice. We may have different roles—some of us may lobby for debt relief; some of us may protest against unjust wars; some of us may donate money to organizations that help political prisoners; some of us may dish out food in a soup kitchen. But all of us should be doing what we can, and the fact of our community means that where you are weak, I can be strong, and vice versa.

U2 helps us understand this, too. The whole band has always supported this peace-and-justice work, even when Bono was the public face of that work. When Bono began working on behalf of Jubilee 2000, for example, a campaign to forgive the debt that cripples Third World nations, the band recognized that this was important work for justice. Millions of people were living in poverty and squalor because their governments—and, sometimes, their corrupt leaders—had accepted international aid that now could only be repaid by keeping entire populations in poverty.

Adam said, "When we heard about Jubilee 2000 we were all on board. We recognized that this was something worth fighting for. We sat down and talked about what we could do as a band but it quickly became apparent that this was a job for one person and the best man for the job was Bono." Larry seconded that; while the band was having to deal with the way it did its work while Bono worked for justice, "nobody could argue with what he was doing, it was clearly too important."[53]

Bono is not, of course, the only member of the band involved in work for peace and justice, and he has not even always been the obvious man for the job. For example, early in the band's history, when Bob Geldof asked U2 to collaborate on a benefit recording for starvation in Ethiopia ("Do They Know It's Christmas"), The Edge and Larry were otherwise occupied, but Bono agreed to sing, and Adam told him, "I'll come and help you out." It was a true media circus, and Bono and Adam were surrounded by a roomful of these monstrously big British pop stars—George Michael, Duran Duran—and were very uncomfortable.

"I knew I was there to chaperone Bono," Adam said. "Bono was the person who had been invited to sing and I understood that he didn't want to go to something like that on his own."[54] In a very real sense, Adam made it possible for Bono to do this recording—which, as we said in chapter 2, is the kind of thing that an *ecclesia* does for its members: it gives them strength and encouragement to do the work they are called to do. And on this occasion, Bono—with Adam's help—sang on a single that raised millions of dollars to help feed starving people in Ethiopia.

I like to think that Jesus approved.

Since that time, U2 has been involved with the LiveAid concert, the Amnesty International tour, and many other causes. Bono's political involvement and organizing savvy have raised awareness of the problems of poverty, AIDS, and Third World debt relief to a level where now millions of people are involved with DATA and the ONE movement, and hundreds of millions of dollars have been raised or budgeted to help feed the hungry, heal the sick, and comfort the suffering. The band's concert and video with Green Day of "The Saints Are Coming" have raised awareness about the suffering that still continues in New Orleans and the Gulf Coast, and The Edge's work with Gibson Guitars for the Music Rising initiative has helped New Orleans musicians who had lost their instruments and their livelihoods after Katrina. The band has recently rolled out a music subscription service that will contribute its profits to peace-and-justice causes, and the members of the band continue to find ways to leverage their fame and fortune to help those whose problems are less known and those who are less fortunate.

"You can't fix every problem," Bono says. "But the ones you can, you must."[55]

They have done much and have inspired others. But there is still more—much more—left to do.

Several years ago, the cover of *Time* magazine asked, "Can Bono Save the World?" It was an audacious question, and one that, of course, can only be answered in the negative, despite all Bono has accomplished. There is more to be done than the members of the world's biggest rock band—and their fans—can ever do. Still, in spite of the challenges, we have a responsibility to act, and in acting, we participate in the life of God, bring the kingdom of God closer, and draw closer to one another and to all those who inhabit our world.

Moreover, not only are we *supposed* to carry one another, we *get* to carry one another. Faith and community should create in us awareness not just of this God-given sense of obligation to work for justice, but also awareness of the joyful privilege of being coworkers with God. This world is in horrible shape—but, thanks be to God, we can do much to make it better, more loving, more grace-filled, in imitation of the God we love and serve.

These actions grow out of beliefs—beliefs we have seen reflected in the music of U2 and explained in interviews they've given over the past three decades. Belief is acted out in community, and belief and community lead to action, and action can change the world:

> One Love, one blood, one life; you got to do what you should . . .
> We get to carry each other, carry each other.

The meaning of life, U2 ultimately reminds us, is not in how much gold you pile up, how many mansions you build, how many people you can order around, or even how loudly and devoutly you pray and proclaim your salvation. It is in what we get to do for each other.

This is U2's faithful message to the world.

Conclusion

Ten Spiritual Lessons from U2

In a book like this, with so many ideas and examples, it can be a challenge sometimes to sum up, even with the core organizing principles of belief, community, and justice to rely on. So to recap our journey, I thought we might pick ten essential spiritual lessons we can learn from U2's life and work, and illustrate each with an apposite line from one of their songs.

1. "But I still haven't found what I'm looking for" (from "I Still Haven't Found What I'm Looking For," *The Joshua Tree*): Life is a journey, not a destination; faith is a means, not an end. It's okay to go on looking, especially if you've got the sense you know which direction you're traveling.

2. "Hello, hello (*¡Hola!*) / I'm at a place called vertigo" (From "Vertigo," *How to Dismantle an Atomic Bomb*): Contemporary life is disconcerting, destabilizing. That is its nature. Don't expect it to be otherwise. That's why we seek meaning from something out-side of all of this chaos—because sometimes it can be so hard to find it in the events of the day-to-day noise and confusion.

3. "We get to carry each other" (from "One," *Achtung Baby*): Our lives are for and with one another. We need one another to be who we are called to be. And not only are we called to carry one another—we are permitted to. It is a grace and a mercy for us as well as for those who need our help.

4. "The goal is elevation" (from "Elevation," *All That You Can't Leave Behind*): We are seeking transcendence for ourselves, our

spirits, our world. We know it when we find it, and for many people, it can be found most reliably in the world of the spirit.

5. "I can't believe the news today / I can't close my eyes and make it go away" (from "Sunday Bloody Sunday," *War*): Ignoring the brokenness we see is not an option; we are called to bring healing and hope, to help transform the world. When good people turn away, in some ways it's worse than the actions of bad people. So however difficult it may be—look. It's the first step in knowing what needs doing.

6. "It's a beautiful day / Don't let it slip away" (from "Beautiful Day," *All That You Can't Leave Behind*): We live in a marvelous creation. Pay attention to it. It's a gift from God, a gift that we'll never have again, and in this gift of beauty, we have an inkling of the God of beauty, the Creator God who gave it to us.

7. "What more in the name of love?" (from "Pride in the Name of Love," *The Unforgettable Fire*): Risk everything for love; there is no higher value. Love changes everything, including us. History shows us that the power of love endures; even after death, love can go on making a difference in the world.

8. "We need love and peace" (from "Love and Peace or Else," *How to Dismantle an Atomic Bomb*): War and cruelty destroy lives and demean the human spirit. We need to seek other solutions than an eye for an eye, and we need to learn to return love for hate, or nothing will ever change.

9. "Sometimes you can't make it on your own" (from "Sometimes You Can't Make It on Your Own," *How to Dismantle an Atomic Bomb*): It's no shame to rely on others. We are made for companionship—especially in tough times. A community—or a dear friend—can make all the difference when we face tragedy, difficulty, or exhaustion.

10. "Walk on" (from "Walk On," *All That You Can't Leave Behind*): Be strong. You can lose everything but what matters most. Don't despair, even when the daylight feels like it's a long way off. Don't stop working for the healing of the world. You are never alone. We are all in this together.

There are other lessons of course, some that we've examined here and many, perhaps, that we haven't, but anyone who walks away from an encounter with U2's music without learning some or all of the lessons above has missed much of what makes the band matter—and continue to matter. As wise spiritual guides and makers of great music, they both entertain us and enlighten us. And who would turn down a bit of elevation, especially when you can dance to it?

Afterword

No Line on the Horizon

In the course of just a few exciting weeks in early 2009, U2 played at a gala concert on the steps of the Lincoln Memorial in Washington, DC, commemorating the inauguration of U.S. president Barack Obama; released a new single, "Get On Your Boots," from the album *No Line on the Horizon*; premiered a new video for the single directed by Alex Courtes; and, at last, released the new album itself, their first in five years. *No Line on the Horizon* is the band's twelfth studio album, and it received immediate acclaim. *Rolling Stone* called *No Line* the band's best album since *Achtung Baby*. Niall Stokes, writing for Ireland's *Hot Press*, said,

> *No Line On The Horizon* is a huge record, full of big songs, powerful riffs and superb musicianship. It's more musically diverse that any U2 album since *Rattle And Hum*, mixing hard rock, psychedelia, pop, electronica, dance, folk, country, spiritual music and orchestral shadings in what is a fantastically heady brew. It will certainly challenge U2 fans, but my guess is that they'll ultimately be inspired. It's going to be a massive record.

Likewise, the *Los Angeles Times* said that *No Line* "is a pilgrimage—the religious metaphor is inevitable—along the path forged by U2 itself."[1]

This album is a great new work—and a welcome one—for a world that desperately needs some good news.

The Obama inauguration was a signal event for Americans and

for people around the world, an event that symbolized a generational shift in direction toward compassion and responsibility. So it seemed only fitting that two musical prophets of doing the right thing—U2 and Bruce Springsteen—should headline the "We Are One" concert that preceded the formal inauguration. At the Lincoln Memorial, where in 1963 their hero Martin Luther King Jr. gave his "I Have a Dream" speech (which Bono referenced as they played "Pride [In the Name of Love],") the band played in the cold January air with warm passion, including a "City of Blinding Lights," which featured Bono repeatedly invoking "blessings not just on the ones who kneel—luckily." U2's participation in this widely seen concert seemed to mark a moment when people were growing aware that the world might be changing—and that the world should be changing—so that nobody was left out.

That awareness was echoed in the first single released from *No Line on the Horizon*, "Get on Your Boots," a call to action from its very first words: "The future needs a big kiss." The song began as something called "Sexy Boots" (the phrase is still repeated several times), but, as The Edge noted, "in the end it was a bit limiting, and so we took it in another direction. That's how it often happens with U2."[2]

And what direction was that? The song can be interpreted in many ways, but in its repeated refrain, "Get on your boots," it reminds us of Bono's prayer breakfast discussion of the moment he began to see that the American church was up to more than he'd ever given it credit for: "These religious guys were willing to get out in the streets, get their boots dirty, wave the placards, follow their convictions with actions . . . making it really hard for people like me to keep their distance. It was amazing. I almost started to like these church people."[3]

"Get on Your Boots" is a similar call to get out in the streets, to follow convictions with actions, but it is also a call for people to refuse to let fear dictate their actions ("Satan loves a bomb scare / But he won't scare you"), to reject war and violence as a solution ("I got a submarine / You got gasoline / I don't want to talk about wars between nations"), and to pull together to do what needs to be done ("Here's where you gotta be / Love and community"). That continues to matter to the band; as a longtime friend of Bono's said to me over a pot of tea in London recently, even after all these years, the most important message of the band is still this: that we get to carry each other.

The video for "Get on Your Boots," which debuted several weeks after the single was released, extends this idea of action and change, although the images pull the lyrics in a slightly different, if equally compelling, direction. As The Edge noted, "[The video is] based around the idea that men have f**ked [sic] things up so badly, politically, economically, and socially, that it's really time we handed things over to women."[4] This idea makes the lines "You don't know how beautiful you are," shown over the images of African mothers and daughters, compelling, and it invites those who have too long been left out of the decision-making process into action.

There's much more in the video, images of explosions and architecture and religious icons coming at us a mile a minute. But the core message emerging from all of this, the music and the moving pictures and the band's performance, seems to be that we are in a time of crisis and that things have got to change—starting with us.

Get on your boots.

The world needs us.

And then, leaked on the Internet and streaming on the band's MySpace page before formally rolling out first in Ireland and then worldwide, was the album itself. The title *No Line on the Horizon*, as we noted earlier, refers to the infinite, to that place where you can't tell the difference between sea and sky, and the album cover comes from a work, "Boden Sea, Uttwil," one of a series of horizon photos by Hiroshi Sugimoto in which the horizon exactly bisects the image. Superimposed over the horizon on the cover is an equals sign (=), which denotes equality, democracy, justice—a number of things that the world needs badly just now.

The album itself is lengthy for a U2 album, around an hour, and at the same time both rock solid and musically adventurous. Producer Brian Eno said in an interview on the U2 Web site that the album reflects Bono's strongest lyrics yet—a continuation of his lyrical artistry that has been evident on at least the previous two albums. Bono lured Eno back to work with them by telling him that they wanted to make a "gospel" album. The final product is—mostly—not a gospel album musically ("Moment of Surrender" might be the exception). It rocks hard, explores ambient sound and trance, and Middle Eastern influences as well—but it is a gospel album lyrically and spiritually, and that is what Bono meant.

The track "Magnificent" encapsulates much of what is good about the album—and much of what we have been saying about U2 and its relationship to faith. In the introduction, I noted how *Rolling Stone* writer Elysa Gardner offered a definition of the band as religious freaks who make some of the world's most compelling music, and this and other tracks on *No Line* offer insight into my ongoing argument that you can't completely understand the music without acknowledging the religion. In his *Rolling Stone* review, David Fricke called "Magnificent" one of several songs on the album that are "singing about singing," and says the song is an anthem to the wonder that the band must feel at still making great music after all these years.[5] Certainly there must be something to that; I think about those Irish twenty-one-year-olds in Oklahoma City all those years ago, and I think how their eyes would twinkle at the thought that the whole world would be listening to them almost thirty years later.

But "Magnifcent" is also a song that—employing the theological filters we have been using throughout the book—reveals itself so clearly as a Christian song of praise (as we defined such things in chapter 1), that to ignore the spiritual dimension of the song is to badly mishear it. "Magnificent" begins simply enough with verses talking about how the singer was born to sing for "you."

Who? A girl?

For us, his audience?

Well, the second verse confirms what religious listeners have already suspected: that the "You" in this song is the One God, the Divine, the Magnificent:

> I didn't have a choice
> But to lift you up
> And sing whatever song you wanted me to.

> I give you back my voice
> From the womb.
> My first cry
> It was a joyful noise.

Knowing Bono's love of the Psalms (and his previous use of them in other songs), these lines immediately suggest his appropriation of Psalm 71: 6 ("Upon you I have leaned from my birth; it was you who took me from my mother's womb. My praise is continually of you") and Psalm 139:13–14a ("For it was you who formed my inward parts; you knit me together in my mother's womb. I praise you, for I am fearfully and wonderfully made"). Meanwhile, that concluding phrase, "joyful noise," appears five times in some of the best-loved psalms, and in each case it is used as here in Psalm 95:1: "O come, let us sing to the LORD; let us make a joyful noise to the rock of our salvation!"

Admittedly many people will listen to "Magnificent" thinking it is joyful noise that has nothing formally religious to it, and they will respond to these deeply theological lines with the secular rapture that they have always found in U2's music:

> Justified till we die
> You and I will magnify
> The Magnificent
> Magnificent

But because in these pages we have identified U2's preoccupation with belief, with praise, with community, and with faithful action, it seems a bit wrong-headed to ignore those things when they are self-evidently present in these songs. For many years I certainly did, and I loved U2's music even when I refused to consider that it might have a sacred dimension. So perhaps it's wrong to suggest secular listeners shouldn't be able to ignore elements of faith in U2's music.

But, I'd suggest, don't imagine that you're really understanding the songs without considering the Christian components in them. To name just a few in *No Line on the Horizon* (an in-depth analysis of the religious and theological in *No Line* would occupy another good-sized chapter and keep this book out of your hands for a long time): In "White as Snow," we find a song about a dying soldier in Afghanistan that "lasts the length of time it takes him to die," according to Bono.[6] "White as Snow" would be one of U2's most powerful and moving songs just on that basis alone. But the tune is also based on the ancient Christmas carol "O Come, O Come, Emmanuel," and the lyrics employ a traditional gospel music trope, "white as snow" (used in many Christian hymns to describe the spotless Lamb of God—or the spotless souls of those forgiven by him), as both the title and repeated chorus of a song that is also about redemption and forgiveness that can come only at the hands of the Son of God we met in chapter 1:

> Once I knew there was a love divine.
> Then came a time I thought it knew me not.
> Who can forgive forgiveness where forgiveness is not?
> Only the lamb as white as snow.

"Moment of Surrender" charts a dark night of the soul worthy of "Wake Up Dead Man," the shouting at God the band explored in *Achtung Baby* or *Pop:*

> I was speeding on the subway
> Through the stations of the cross
> Every eye looking every other way
> Counting down 'til the pain will stop.

It is only at the moment of surrender, when the singer drops to his knees, that he can find what he is looking for.

In "Stand Up Comedy," the singer affirms, "I can stand up for hope, faith, love," a phrase echoing the apostle Paul, who describes these as the central Christian virtues in 1 Corinthians 13:13 ("And now faith, hope, and love abide, these three; and the greatest of these is love").

"Unknown Caller" is a tale of redemption for the computer age:

> Restart and re-boot yourself
> You're free to go
> Oh, oh
> Shout for joy if you get the chance
> Password, you, enter here, right now

This could of course simply refer to your everyday secular redemption: Find Yourself. Live your Bliss. But the song also suggests in twenty-first-century text-speak the presence of a presence (a Presence), perhaps even the Yahweh we encountered earlier in the book:

> Hear me, cease to speak that I may speak
> Shush now
> Oh, oh
> Then don't move or say a thing

This sounds very like the Living God speaking out in another of Bono's Psalms:

> "Be still, and know that I am God!
>   I am exalted among the nations,
>   I am exalted in the earth."
>   (Ps. 46:10)

There's more—much more. But it's clear from these examples that in many of the songs on *No Line on the Horizon,* Bono continues the practice he followed on *All that You Can't Leave Behind* and *How to Dismantle an Atomic Bomb* of dealing expressly with religious and spiritual impulses. This, of course, is something U2 has done in one fashion or other since the very beginning. On my most recent trip to England, I ran across a 1984 British interview of The Edge about the spiritual content of U2's music. "It's not just the fact that it's there," The Edge said then, addressing some of the band's detractors. "It's the way it's presented in an extremely challenging, extremely powerful way. It demands a response, and I don't think people generally like that."[7]

Well, it still demands a response, but people have gotten used to it by now; in fact, as we said, after 9/11, people actually began to look to U2 for spiritual guidance. Their concerts became healing services and peace and justice rallies for hundreds of thousands, and their music on the radio brought comfort and hope to millions. And now, as I write in early 2009, with the world's economies in shambles, uncertainty in the Middle East and Korea, the environment degraded, and many things seemingly falling to pieces, people still need U2—not the naive but earnest boys of the 1980s, not the ironic rock icons of the 1990s, but the grizzled veterans of Amnesty and Live-Aid and DATA and the ONE Movement. They need the present-day U2 that has walked a long hard road and fought the good fight and is still making music that matters— music that calls for us to fight the good fight alongside them. In "I'll Go Crazy If I Don't Go Crazy Tonight," Bono sings, "Every generation has a chance to change the world," and this may indeed be our moment. And if it is, we'll get on our boots, turn up our music, and head out into the streets to make a difference.

Don't be surprised if—there at the front of the parade—we see a scrappy little Irishman decked out in shades and leather, waving a white flag, singing his guts out.

Of course, if that happens, we'll also see three of his mates, pushing, shoving, urging him—and us—along too.

Notes

Introduction: The Gospel according to U2

1. Lyrics quoted from the band's albums and singles are drawn from the band's Web site, u2.com, with the proviso that even they may sometimes represent the band's best guess. Bono, the primary lyricist for the band, has been said to speak in a foreign language, Bongelese, when he's creating lyrics. When I am quoting Bono's lyrical divergences or verbal ramblings in concerts, I will likewise be using my best guess. I will be summarizing and paraphrasing lyrics throughout, since fair-use standards for critical works such as this do not permit quotation of entire songs. Consult the U2 site for complete lyrics.

2. Elysa Gardner, introduction to *U2: The Rolling Stone Files*, ed. *Rolling Stone Magazine* (New York: Hyperion, 1994), xi.

3. As we'll note, three of the band members (Bono, The Edge, and Larry Mullen Jr.) were once part of the same charismatic Christian community in Dublin; Adam Clayton might be (and often is) described as spiritual but not religious.

4. "Thomas Kinkade the Artist," http://www.thomaskinkade.com/magi/servlet/com.asucon.ebiz.biography.web.tk.BiographyServlet.

5. H. Richard Niebuhr, *Christ and Culture* (1951; repr., New York: Harper & Row, 1975), 40. I say "so-called," in relation to secular culture because as I'll argue later, I subscribe to the incarnational and sacramental notion that in a world created by God and redeemed by Christ, God can be seen, heard, and felt moving in ways outside the walls of the church and the official sacraments of the church—the notion that, as N. T. Wright says, "The present world really is a signpost to a larger beauty, a deeper truth." Not the whole truth, certainly. But an arrow pointing in the direction of what really matters (N. T. Wright, *Simply Christian: Why Christianity Makes Sense* [New York: HarperCollins, 2006], 47).

6. Stuart Bailie and Hugh Linehan, "Saints or Sinners?" *The Irish Times*, Aug. 19, 2008, http://www.irishtimes.com/newspaper/theticket/2008/0718/121 6073230687.html.

7. Eamon Dunphy, *Unforgettable Fire* (New York: Warner Books, 1988), 81.

8. Michka Assayas, *Bono in Conversation with Michka Assayas* (New York: Riverhead, 2005), 14.

9. "A Social History of U2: 1976–2005," *The Dubliner*, June 2005, http://the dubliner.typepad.com/the_dubliner_magazine/2007/04/a_social_histor.html .

10. Bono, The Edge, Adam Clayton, and Larry Mullen Jr., with Neil McCormick, *U2 by U2*, (New York: HarperEntertainment, 2006), 228.

11. Ibid., 269.

12. Diana Butler Bass, *Christianity for the Rest of Us: How the Neighborhood Church Is Transforming the Faith* (New York: HarperOne, 2006), 57.

13. Mike Kalil, "The Church of Bono," *Las Vegas Review-Journal*, Nov. 4, 2005, http://www.atu2.com/news/article.src?ID=4110&Key=&Year=&Cat=5.

14. "U2 Scrap Rick Rubin Tracks on New Album," *NME*, Nov. 26, 2008, http://www.nme.com/news/u2/41303.

15. Bono et. al., *U2 by U2*, 8.

16. James Henke, "U2: Here Comes the 'Next Big Thing': Future Looks Bright for Irish Rockers," *Rolling Stone*, Feb. 19, 1981, http://www.rollingstone .com/artists/u2/articles/story/7088993/u2_here_comes_the_next_big_thing.

17. Ibid., 6.

18. Dunphy, *Unforgettable Fire*, 234.

19. Paul Vallely, "Bono the Missionary," *The Independent*, May 13, 2006, http://www.independent.co.uk/news/people/bono-the-missionary-477945.html.

20. Bono et. al, *U2 by U2*, 177.

21. David Fricke, "U2 Dissect 'Bomb': Bono, Edge, Adam and Larry Have Their Say," *Rolling Stone*, Dec. 15, 2004, http://www.rollingstone.com/news/ story/6769075/u2_dissect_bomb.

22. Assayas, *Bono in Conversation*, 51.

23. And literally that is what the word means, "speaking about God."

24. Rowan Williams, *On Christian Theology* (Malden, MA: Blackwell, 2000), xi.

25. Jay Cocks, "Band on the Run, *Time*, Apr. 27, 1987, http://www.time .com/time/magazine/article/0,9171,964182,00.html.

26. Eugene Peterson, foreword to *Get Up Off Your Knees: Preaching the U2 Catalog*, ed. Raewynne J. Whiteley and Beth Maynard (Boston: Cowley, 2003), xi.

27. Kelton Cobb, introduction to *The Blackwell Guide to Theology and Popular Culture* (Malden, MA: Blackwell, 2005), 7.

28. H. Niebuhr, *Christ and Culture*, 192; Paul Tillich, "Aspects of a Religious Analysis of Culture," in *The Essential Tillich*, ed. F. Forrester Church (1987; repr., Chicago: University of Chicago Press, 1999), 110.

29. Christopher Connelly, "Keeping the Faith," in *U2*, 35.

30. "Bono in San Antonio," *U2 Magazine* 3, May 1, 1982, http://u2_interviews .tripod.com/id14.html.

31. Jason Byassee, "Review of *One Step Closer: Why U2 Matters to Those Seeking God*," *Christian Century*, Aug. 8, 2006, http://www.christiancentury.org/ article.lasso?id=2261.

32. N. T. Wright, "Resurrection: From Theology to Music and Back Again," in *Sounding the Depths: Theology through the Arts* (London: SCM Press, 2002), 210–11.

Chapter One: Belief

1. Bono, *On the Move: A Speech* (Nashville: W Publishing Group, 2006), 50. Bono's speech/homily at the 54th National Prayer Breakfast is also widely available on the Web, but all royalties from this beautiful little book go to the ONE Project.

2. George Appleton, ed., introduction to *The Oxford Book of Prayer* (Oxford: Oxford University Press, 1985), x.

3. John Bunyan, *Prayer* (Edinburgh: Banner of Truth, 1965), 13.

4. In addition to Psalm 40, Bono also cribbed a line from Psalm 6, which he likewise used in "New Year's Day": "How long to sing this song?"

5. Bono, "Psalm Like It Hot," *The Observer*, Oct. 31, 1999, http://www .guardian.co.uk/theobserver/1999/oct/31/featuresreview.review2.

6. Ibid.

7. Thomas Merton, *New Seeds of Contemplation* (1961; repr., Boston: Shambhala, 2003), 47.

8. Bono et. al., *U2 by U2*, 266.

9. Ibid.

10. Augustine, *Enarrationes in Psalmos* 32.8.

11. I like to think that Augustine would have liked *October*. He was inordinately fond of music for both its beauty and its spiritual value. He once preached that "to sing once is to pray twice." Augustine, *Sermones* 336.1 PL 38, 1472.

12. Walter Brueggemann, *Mandate to Difference: An Invitation to the Contemporary Church* (Louisville, KY: Westminster John Knox Press, 2007), 1.

13. Rowan Williams, "The Spiritual and the Religious: Is the Territory Changing?" lecture, Westminster Cathedral, London, April 17, 2008, http://www .archbishopofcanterbury.org/1759.

14. Bono et. al., *U2 by U2*, 9.

15. Henry O. Thompson, s.v. "Yahweh," *Anchor Bible Dictionary*. CD-ROM, New York: Doubleday, 1999.

16. Desmond Tutu, *God Has a Dream: A Vision of Hope for Our Time* (New York: Image, 2004), viii.

17. Bono, *On the Move*, 16.

18. Brueggemann, *Mandate to Difference*, 3.

19. Desmond Tutu, *Hope and Suffering* (Grand Rapids: Wm. B. Eerdmans Publishing Co., 1984), 51.

20. Jane Lampman, "Evangelicals Find the Center," *Christian Science Monitor*, Mar. 19, 2008, http://features.csmonitor.com/books/2008/03/19/evangelicals -find-the-center-2/.

21. Jeremy Begbie, "Sound Theology," *The Christian Century* 124, no. 23 (2007):20(6). *General OneFile*, Gale, Baylor University, Dec. 10, 2007.

22. Jeremy Begbie, "Music in God's World," *Books & Culture* 13, no. 5 (2007), http://www.christianitytoday.com/bc/2007/005/10.28.html.

23. Michka Assayas, *Bono in Conversation with Michka Assayas* (New York: Riverhead, 2005), 125; for Augustine on divine love manifested through the incarnation, see *De Trinitate* 15.17, 31.

24. Karl Barth, *Church Dogmatics: The Doctrine of God* (Edinburgh: T. & T. Clark, 1957), 509.

25. Assayas, *Bono in Conversation*, 200.

26. Greg Garrett, *Stories from The Edge: A Theology of Grief* (Louisville, KY: Westminster John Knox Press, 2008), 83.

27. Assayas, *Bono in Conversation*, 125.

28. Ibid., 85. "Liberating king" is one way to translate the ancient title "Christ," which some people think is Jesus' last name: Jesus Christ. Jesus *is* the Christ, the Greek equivalent of the Jewish word "messiah," which describes the king sent by God to liberate his people.

29. Athanasius, *St. Athanasius on the Incarnation: The Treatise* De Incarnatione Verbi Dei, (London: A. R. Mowbray, 1963), 26; Thomas Aquinas, *Summa Theologaie: A Concise Translation*, ed. Timothy McDermott (Westminster, MD: Christian Classics, 1989), 475.

30. Assayas, *Bono in Conversation*, 204. "The obvious death" is probably Bono referring to Rom. 6:23: "For the wages of sin is death, but the free gift of God is eternal life in Christ Jesus our Lord."

31. Peter Abailard, "Exposition of the Epistle to the Romans," in *A Scholastic Miscellany: Anselm to Ockham*, vol. 10, Library of Christian Classics, trans. Gerald E. Moffat (Philadelphia: Westminster Press, 1956), 283.

32. Brian D. McLaren, *Everything Must Change: Jesus, Global Crises, and a Revolution of Hope* (Nashville: Thomas Nelson, 2008), 79.

33. Brian McLaren, *The Secret Message of Jesus* (Nashville: Thomas Nelson, 2006), 60.

34. David Breskin, "Bono: The Rolling Stone Interview," in *U2: The Rolling Stone Files*, ed. *Rolling Stone Magazine* (New York: Hyperion, 1994), 96.

35. Gustavo Gutiérrez, *On Job: God-Talk and the Suffering of the Innocent*, trans. Matthew J. O'Connell (Maryknoll, NY: Orbis Books, 1987), 90.

36. Rowan Williams, *On Christian Theology* (Oxford: Blackwell, 2000), 107.

37. Steve Stockman, *Walk On: The Spiritual Journey of U2* (Orlando: Relevant, 2005), 23.

38. Bill Graham and Caroline van Oosten de Boer, *The Complete Guide to the Music of U2*, 2nd ed. (London: Omnibus Press, 2004), 22.

39. Cathleen Falsani, "Bono's American Prayer," *Christianity Today*, March 2003, http://www.christianitytoday.com/ct/2003/march/2.38.htm.

40. Demetrios J. Constantelos, "Eastern Orthodoxy and the Bible," *The Oxford Guide to the Bible*, ed. Bruce M. Metzger and Michael D. Coogan (New York: Oxford, 1993), 174.

41. Bono et. al., *U2 by U2*, 221.

42. Ibid., 248.

43. Jürgen Moltmann, *History and the Triune God: Contributions to Trinitarian Theology* (New York: Crossroad, 1992), 65.

44. Bono et. al., *U2 by U2*, 136.

45. "U2 Scrap Rick Rubin Tracks," *NME*.

46. Moltmann, *History*, 59.

47. Ibid., 63.

Chapter Two: Communion

1. Bono, The Edge, Adam Clayton, and Larry Mullen Jr., with Neil McCormick, *U2 by U2* (New York: HarperEntertainment, 2006), 307.

2. David Breskin, "Bono: The Rolling Stone Interview," in *U2: The Rolling Stone Files*, ed. *Rolling Stone Magazine* (New York: Hyperion, 1994), 96.

3. Mark LePage, "Bass Notes: U2's Adam Clayton on Geography, Spirituality and Rock 'n' Roll," *Montreal Gazette*, May 26, 2001, http://www.atu2.com/news/article.src?ID=1161&Key=&Year=&Cat=.

4. Brian McLaren, "Why Bother With Church at All?" http://www.brianmclaren.net/archives/faq/why-bother-with.html (accessed March 17, 2009).

5. David Fricke, "U2 Finds What It's Looking For," in *U2*, 188.

6. David Kinnaman and Gabe Lyons, *unChristian: What a New Generation Thinks about Christianity . . . And Why It Matters* (Grand Rapids: Baker, 2007) 15, 18.

7. Rowan Williams, "The Spiritual and the Religious: Is the Territory Changing?" Westminster Cathedral, London, Apr. 17, 2008, http://www.archbishopofcanterbury.org/1759.

8. Jay Cocks, "Band on the Run," *Time,* Apr. 27, 1987, http://www.time.com/time/magazine/article/0,9171,964182,00.html.

9. Steve Stockman, *Walk On: The Spiritual Journey of U2* (Orlando: Relevant, 2005), 2.

10. "Bono's Thin Ecclesiology," *Christianity Today*, March 2003, http://www.christianitytoday.com/ct/2003/march/29.37.html.

11. Brian D. McLaren, *Everything Must Change: Jesus, Global Crisis, and a Revolution of Hope* (Grand Rapids: Zondervan, 2008), 299.

12. Samuel T. Lloyd III, "Practicing the Hope of the World," *Cathedral Voice*, September 2008, 1.

13. Chrissy Illey, "U2 Interview: Group Therapy," *The Sunday Times,* Nov. 7, 2004, http://www.timesonline.co.uk/tol/life_and_style/article500245.ece.

14. Jay Cocks, "Band on the Run," *Time,* Apr. 27, 1987, http://www.time.com/time/magazine/article/0,9171,964182,00.html.

15. Bono et. al., *U2 by U2*, 8.

16. Illey, "U2 Interview."

17. Bono et. al., *U2 by U2*, 7.

18. Jürgen Moltmann, *History and the Triune God: Contributions to Trinitarian Theology* (New York: Crossroad, 1992), xii/xiii, 64.

19. Martin Luther King Jr., *Strength to Love* (1963; repr., Philadelphia: Fortress Press, 1981), 49–51.

20. David Fricke, "U2 Dissect 'Bomb,'" *Rolling Stone,* Dec. 15, 2004, http://www.rollingstone.com/artists/u2/articles/story/6769075/u2_dissect_bomb.

21. "Bono Bites Back," *Mother Jones,* May 1, 1989, http://www.mother jones.com/arts/books/1989/05/bono.html.

22. Bono et. al., *U2 by U2,* 72.

23. Ibid.

24. Illey, "U2 Interview."

25. Bono et. al., *U2 by U2,* 117.

26. "Bono Bites Back."

27. Bono et. al., *U2 by U2,* 118.

28. Ibid., 119.

29. Michka Assayas, *Bono in Conversation with Michka Assayas* (New York: Riverhead, 2005), 168.

30. Anthony DeCurtis, "Zoo World Order," in *U2,* 216–17.

31. Bono et al., *U2 by U2,* 7.

32. Ibid., 164.

33. Ibid., 256.

34. Michael Oliveira, "Daniel Lanois Says New U2 Album Is 'Fantastically Innovative'," *The Canadian Press,* Nov. 4, 2008, http://www.atu2.com/news/article.src?ID=5124.

35. Tom Wright, *Matthew for Everyone: Part Two* (Louisville, KY: Westminster John Knox Press, 2004), 36.

36. Fricke, "U2 Dissect 'Bomb'."

37. Assayas, *Bono in Conversation,* 123.

38. Bono et. al., *U2 by U2,* 256.

39. Austin Scaggs, "The Police Say Farewell With New York Blowout," *Rolling Stone,* Sept. 4, 2008, http://www.rollingstone.com/artists/thepolice/articles/story/22682497/the_police_say_farewell_with_new_york_blowout.

40. Bruce Springsteen, "Farewell to Danny," Apr. 25, 2008, http://www.brucespringsteen.net/news/index.html.

41. Bono et. al., *U2 by U2,* 345.

42. Assayas, *Bono in Conversation,* 121–22.

43. Desmond Tutu, *God Has a Dream: A Vision of Hope for Our Time* (New York: Image, 2004), 25.

44. Stanley Hauerwas, *A Community of Character: Toward a Constructive Christian Social Ethic* (Notre Dame, IN: University of Notre Dame Press, 1982), 3.

45. Fricke, "U2 Dissect 'Bomb'."

46. Beth Maynard, "Respect, Righteousness and a Mirrorball Lemon: A Response to *Christianity Today*'s Editorial on Bono," in *Thunderstruck,* http://www.thunderstruck.org/maynard.htm (accessed March 17, 2009).

47. Assayas, *Bono in Conversation,* 201.

Chapter Three: Social Justice

1. Brian D. McLaren, *Everything Must Change: Jesus, Global Crisis, and a Revolution of Hope* (Grand Rapids: Zondervan, 2008), 5–6. Brian's book is, in part, an attempt to examine these framing stories and tell new ones that are closer to the spirit of the narrative Jesus lived.

2. Bono, *On the Move: A Speech* (Nashville: W Publishing Group, 2006), 16, 18–19.

3. Bill Gates, "Making Capitalism More Creative," *Time*, Jul. 31, 2008, http://www.time.com/time/business/article/0,8599,1828069,00.html.

4. Scot McKnight, *The Blue Parakeet: Rethinking How You Read the Bible*, (Grand Rapids: Zondervan, 2008), 13.

5. Phyllis Tickle, *The Great Emergence: How Christianity Is Changing and Why* (Grand Rapids: Baker, 2008), 91.

6. "About Focus on the Family," http://www.focusonthefamily.com/about _us.aspx (accessed March 17, 2009).

7. David Breskin, "Bono: The Rolling Stone Interview," in *U2: The Rolling Stone Files*, ed. *Rolling Stone Magazine* (New York: Hyperion, 1994), 97.

8. Michka Assayas, *Bono in Conversation with Michka Assayas* (New York: Riverhead, 2005), 254.

9. Brian D. McLaren, *Finding Our Way Again: The Return of the Ancient Practices* (Nashville: Thomas Nelson, 2008), 114–15.

10. Assayas, *Bono in Conversation*, 167. Bono refers to a scene found in the various Gospels that is the inauguration of Jesus' public ministry in the Gospel of John (John 2:13–16).

11. *The Oxford Companion to the Bible*, ed. Bruce M. Metzger and Michael D. Coogan (New York: Oxford, 1993), 405.

12. David Heim, "Breakfast with Bono," *Christian Century,* Mar. 21, 2006, 21.

13. Bono et. al., *U2 by U2*, 186.

14. Martin Luther King Jr., "Letter from a Birmingham Jail," in *I Have a Dream: Writings and Speeches that Changed the World*, ed. James M. Washington (New York: HarperCollins, 1992), 95.

15. Rabbi Joseph Telushkin, *Biblical Literacy: The Most Important People, Events, and Ideas of the Hebrew Bible* (New York: William Morrow, 1997), 299.

16. Bono et. al., *U2 by U2*, 184. Sting wrote a similar song, "Gueca Solo," around the same time as *The Joshua Tree* was released about a widespread silent protest in Chile where women danced silently with photos of their missing sons, husbands, and fathers as armed soldiers looked on.

17. Ibid., 184.

18. Anthony DeCurtis, "Truths and Consequences," in *U2*, 69.

19. Bono et. al., *U2 by U2*, 179.

20. DeCurtis, "Truths and Consequences," 69.

21. Eugene Peterson, foreword to *Get Up Off Your Knees: Preaching the U2 Catalog,* ed. Raewynne J. Whiteley and Beth Maynard (Boston: Cowley, 2003), xii.

22. Parke Puterbaugh, "Performance Review," in *U2*, 174.

23. Bono et. al., *U2 by U2*, 248.

24. David Fricke, "U2 Finds What It's Looking For," in *U2*, 179.

25. N. T. Wright, *Simply Christian: Why Christianity Makes Sense* (New York: HarperSanFancisco, 2006), 13.

26. *Oxford Companion*, 408; Dennis C. Duling, "The Kingdom of God:" *The Anchor Bible Dictionary*, electronic version.

27. Steve Stockman, "Pressing On with U2 and Paul," in *Get Up Off Your Knees*, 88.

28. Rowan Williams, *Tokens of Trust: An Introduction to Christian Belief* (Louisville, KY: Westminster John Knox Press, 2007), 58.

29. Rowan Williams, *On Christian Theology* (Malden, MA: Blackwell, 2000), 255.

30. Martin Luther King Jr., "On Being a Good Neighbor," in *Strength to Love* (1963; repr., Philadelphia: Fortress Press, 1981), 33.

31. Bono et. al., *U2 by U2*, 337.

32. Assayas, *Bono in Conversation*, 203.

33. Bono et. al., *U2 by U2*, 299.

34. Wright, *Simply Christian*, 10.

35. Marcus Borg, *The Heart of Christianity: Rediscovering a Life of Faith* (New York: HarperSanFrancisco, 2003), 178–79; McKnight, *The Blue Parakeet*, 112; McLaren, *Everything Must Change*, 94.

36. The literature on suffering and faith is extensive. For more information, I'd encourage you to look at my short book *Stories from The Edge: A Theology of Grief* (Louisville, KY: Westminster John Knox Press, 2008), which examines a number of the stories we tell about suffering, suggests possible meanings, and might lead you on to other resources if you're so inclined.

37. Williams, *Tokens of Trust*, 44, 48.

38. Assayas, *Bono in Conversation*, 85.

39. King, *Strength to Love*, 102.

40. Bono et. al., *U2 by U2*, 325.

41. King, "Letter," 97.

42. Martin Luther King Jr., "The Drum Major Instinct," in *I Have a Dream*, 191.

43. Bono et. al., *U2 by U2*, 155. Bono refers to the murder of Abel by his brother Cain in the book of Genesis: "And the LORD said, 'What have you done? Listen; your brother's blood is crying out to me from the ground!' " (Gen. 4:10).

44. Gustavo Gutierrez, *A Theology of Liberation: History, Politics, and Salvation*, trans. and ed. Caridad Inda and John Eagleson (Maryknoll, NY: Orbis Books, 1973), 45.

45. Ibid., 199.

46. Leonardo Boff, *Jesus Christ Liberator: A Critical Christology for Our Time*, trans. Patrick Hughes (Maryknoll, NY: Orbis Books, 1978), 112–13.

47. "Bono: The Rolling Stone Interview," in *U2*, 96–97.

48. Assayas, *Bono in Conversation*, 123.

49. Bono et. al., *U2 by U2*, 324–35.

50. Desmond Tutu, *God Has a Dream: A Vision of Hope for Our Time* (New York, Image, 2004), 62.

51. Breskin, "Bono: The Rolling Stone Interview," 96.

52. Josh Tyrangiel, "Bono's Mission," *Time*, Feb.23, 2002, http://www.time.com/time/magazine/article/0,9171,1001931,00.html.

53. Bono et. al., *U2 by U2*, 293.

54. Ibid., 158.

55. Assayas, *Bono in Conversation*, 83.

Afterword: No Line on the Horizon

1. David Fricke, "No Line on the Horizon," *Rolling Stone,* Feb. 20, 2009, http://www.rollingstone.com/reviews/album/26079033/review/26212378/no_line_on_the_horizon; Ann Powers, "'No Line on the Horizon' by U2," *Los Angeles Times*, Feb. 25, 2009, http://www.latimes.com/entertainment/la-et-u2-25-2009feb25,0,5086372.story; "Ireland Leads the Way with New U2 Album," *Hot Press*, Jan. 26, 2009, www.hotpress.com/news/5225641.html.

2. "Ireland Leads the Way."

3. Bono, *On the Move: A Speech* (Nashville: W. Publishing, 2006), 10.

4. "Ireland Leads the Way."

5. Fricke, "No Line on the Horizon."

6. Sean O'Hagen, "White As Snow: U2's Most Intimate Song," *The Guardian*, Feb. 13, 2009, http://www.guardian.co.uk/music/musicblog/2009/feb/13/u2-white-as-snow.

7. Tony Fletcher, "The Pride of Lions: Pt. Two," *Jamming!* October 1984, 32.

Acknowledgments

My friend and theology teacher Anthony Baker recently gave a talk where he recounted a question he had been asked in class—not by me, I'm pleased to note—that stopped him in his tracks: "What kind of theology is this?"

He didn't know how to respond, although he thought about answering the question in this way: "Christian theology."

That's how I think I would answer any similar questions about the methodology of this book: I'm trying to do Christian theology, as I understand Christianity and theology. By inclination and past history, I'm interested in the methodologies of *narratology*—what are the stories we find here, how are they shaped, and what do they teach us?—and *cultural studies*—how can we approach these cultural artifacts as texts and what do they teach us about the culture they represent?—but I'm most interested in having a conversation about the Bible, God, and Christian praxis that includes contemporary theologians and Bible scholars and Augustine and Anselm and Thomas Aquinas and desert fathers and mothers and Martin Luther King Jr. and U2. So if there is a system here, it's an attempt to extract spiritual meanings from the music and lives of U2 and to explore those meanings with the help of a lot of people who have done or are doing theology.

That means there are an awful lot of people to thank.

First and foremost, I must thank those theologians Bono, The Edge, Larry Mullen Jr., and Adam Clayton for the work and the faithful lives this book discusses. I've been listening to U2 for almost thirty years; playing their songs for eight; and reading about them, listening to their music, and thinking about them daily

137

for the past two years. It's unusual for me to come to the end of a nonfiction book project with more passion for the subject than I had when I began it, but that is how I have felt as I put the finishing touches on this book. I am more interested in U2—and more passionate about their music and their work for peace and justice—than ever. So thanks to them, and also to all those who make their work possible.

I'm also grateful to all those over the years who have interviewed or written about U2. Two works were invaluable for me and would also be for anyone writing about U2 from now on: *U2 by U2*, the mammoth book-length interview of all four members of the band and Paul McGuiness conducted by Neil McCormick, and *Bono*, the book-length interview done by Michka Assayas. Many years have passed since I met U2 in the early 1980s, but because of the incredible volume of material written about them, there was little I could imagine asking them that had not already been covered by someone, somewhere, since then. I am grateful to the fan sites, particularly the monumental @U2, and the official U2 Web site, U2.com, which I used for breaking news and "official" lyrics.

Many thanks to Brian McLaren, one of the busiest people I know, for taking time out of his schedule to write the foreword to this book. Our love for U2 is one of several shared passions (as you may gather from my many references to his books). I'm thankful both for his contribution to this volume and for his ongoing commitment to speaking and writing about what a vibrant and authentic Christianity might look like in the twenty-first century.

It is, as ever, great fun to work with the publishing professionals at Westminster John Knox Press, who know how to put out a good book and how to throw a good party. I am grateful to my editor and friend, David Dobson, who asked me to write this book; to my publicist, Emily Kiefer, who somehow always manages to make me look good; and to my editor at The Thoughtful Christian, David Maxwell. I'm also grateful to all the WJK staff—editorial, sales, and fulfillment—who get my books out and into the hands of readers. In the UK, I thank my European publicist Elaine Reed at Alban Books.

I have taught at Baylor University for twenty years now, and I am grateful for the support of its administration, particularly former provost Randall O'Brian, my dean Lee Nordt, my former department chair Maurice Hunt, and my present chair Dianna Vitanza. This book was written during a university research leave in 2008, and could not have been written without that gift of extended time and focus. I also give thanks for my students at Baylor, who keep teaching me new things.

Friends, teachers, pastors, priests, bishops (and archbishops) have talked with me about U2, theology, music, and life over the years: Chris Seay, Philip and Ali Newell, Scott Walker, Tom Hanks, Blake Burleson, Roger Paynter, Rowan Williams, Frank Griswold, Greg Rickel, Andy Doyle, Brian McLaren, Phyllis Tickle, Hulitt Gloer, Hunt Priest, Roger Joslin, Cathy Boyd, Don Smith, Lisa Hines, Kevin Schubert, Carissa Baldwin, Heath Abel, Ken Malcolm, and Joe Behen. I give thanks for you all.

I'm thankful for my boys, Jake and Chandler.

I am thankful for Martha Salazar, to whom this book is dedicated. I hope she knows my love and appreciation. Her support and encouragement help make books like this one possible.

Thanks to the Seminary of the Southwest in Austin, Texas, where I was trained as a theologian and where I continue to be a part of a special community. Thanks to SSW's dean, Doug Travis, to Tony Baker, Cynthia Briggs Kittredge, Ray Pickett, Steve Bishop, Charlie Cook, Alan Gregory, Nathan Jennings, and Bob Kinney, and to Edwin Beckham and Stephen Kidd, who were my research assistants for this book.

I worship, lead retreats, preach, and teach at St. David's Episcopal Church in Austin, Texas. I am grateful for its rector the Rev. David Boyd, and for the Revs. Ken Malcolm, Ron Smith, Chad Vaughn, and Mary Vano, and for all the parishioners who make St. David's special. I also give thanks for St. James Episcopal Church in Austin, and Calvary Episcopal Church, Bastrop, Texas, two *ecclesias* that have been instrumental in my life and work. I am, as always, grateful to the Rt. Rev. Greg Rickel, bishop of Olympia, who steered me in the direction of the life I now live.

This book was researched, written, and edited at Baylor University in Waco, Texas; at Canterbury Cathedral in Canterbury,

England; at the Seminary of the Southwest in Austin, Texas; at the Casa del Sol retreat center at Ghost Ranch, in Abiquiu, New Mexico; at the National Cathedral in Washington, DC, where I was the Fall 2008 Cathedral College Fellow; and at the Hill Country cabin of Hulitt Gloer outside Kerrville, Texas. At Canterbury, I was welcomed by the libraries and the staff of the International Study Center; at SSW, thanks go to Alan Gregory and John Bennet Waters for my office and for research assistance; at Ghost Ranch, I thank Gary Salazar, who took care of a snowed-in writer during the final stages of the writing of this book, Carole Landess at the Casa del Sol retreat center, and my friend and benefactor Jim Baird; at the Cathedral College, I was hosted by Shelagh Casey Brown, Wanda Rixon, and Joan Roberts, and welcomed by all the staff of that late great institution, as well as by Lucy Hogan at Wesley Seminary. Thanks to all of you. This is a better book because I had blessed places to write it.

I couldn't write books like this without Accordance, the best dang Bible software in the whole world. Thanks to all of you at Oak Tree Software for continually making Accordance more useful.

I discovered while I was writing this book that The Edge and I both play Taylor acoustic guitars, Fender Stratocasters, and Epiphone Casinos. Of course, The Edge seems to play every guitar known to humankind, so this may not be a moment of mystical communion or anything like that. Still, I remain open to that possibility.

I want to say thanks, finally, to you for reading this book. I hope and pray that it has been both of interest and of use to you. My prayer to Yahweh for all of us is this:

> Take this soul
> Stranded in some skin and bones.
> Take this soul
> And make it sing.

Greg Garrett
Casa del Sol, Ghost Ranch
Abiquiu, New Mexico
Christmas 2008

About the Author

Greg Garrett is the author of *The Gospel according to Hollywood*, *The Gospel Reloaded* (with Chris Seay), *Holy Superheroes*, and *Stories from The Edge: A Theology of Grief*; of the critically acclaimed novels *Free Bird* (named by *Publishers Weekly* and the *Denver Rocky Mountain News* as one of the best first novels of 2002), *Cycling*, and *Shame*; and of the memoirs *Crossing Myself* and *No Idea*. Greg is also the translator of Mark, Hebrews, 1 and 2 Samuel, Amos, Micah, and other books of the Bible for The Voice Scripture project. He has written on narrative, culture, religion, and politics for print and Web publications, including *Poets & Writers*, *Christianity Today*, *Society of Biblical Literature Forum*, *Utne*, *Relevant*, *Ethics Daily*, and The Thoughtful Christian, and is a featured blogger for *The Christian Century* at theotherjesus.com.

Greg is Professor of English at Baylor University in Waco, Texas, where he has received university-wide teaching honors from both the administration and the student congress. At Baylor, he teaches undergraduate and graduate classes in creative writing, American literature, film, and theology and literature. He is a licensed lay preacher in the Episcopal Church and serves the church as Writer in Residence to the priests and pastors in training at the Seminary of the Southwest in Austin, Texas. Greg regularly teaches, gives readings, lectures, and leads workshops and retreats across the United States and overseas, and is a frequent media guest who has appeared on National Public Radio, CBS Radio, BBC Radio, and the Bob Edwards Show. He lives in Austin with his sons Jake and Chandler.

Related Books from Westminster John Knox Press

The Gospel according to Bruce Springsteen
Rock and Redemption, from *Asbury Park*
to *Magic*
By Jeffrey B. Symynkywicz
ISBN: 978-0-664-23169-9

The Gospel according to the Beatles
By Steve Turner
ISBN: 978-0-664-22983-2

The Gospel according to *The Simpsons***, Bigger**
and Perhaps Even Better! Edition
The Spiritual Life of the World's Most
Animated Family
By Mark I. Pinsky
ISBN: 978-0-664-23160-6

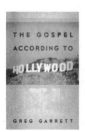

The Gospel according to Hollywood
By Greg Garrett
ISBN: 978-0-664-23052-4

Available everywhere books are sold.